TESTING COLOURS

BRITISH TEST, TRIALS AND RESEARCH AIRCRAFT OF A&AEE, RAE & ETPS SINCE 1960

Royal Aircraft Establishment

TESTING COLOURS

BRITISH TEST, TRIALS AND RESEARCH AIRCRAFT OF A&AEE, RAE & ETPS SINCE 1960

ADRIAN M. BALCH

ACKNOWLEDGEMENTS

I would like to thank the many people who have made this book possible, but special thanks should go to the following, who have helped in various ways: Squadron Leader John Taylor, A&AEE Public Relations Officer; David Horner, formerly RAE Public Relations Officer; Wally Drew and Bob Reed of DRA. Bedford's Photographic Department; Peter Cooper, Peter Middlebrook, Ray Thompson, Sue and Bill Bushell, International Air Tattoo Press Officers and photographers whose names are credited alongside the pictures. This was originally going to be a book of black and white photographs with a few pages of colour and my apologies go to those friends who supplied many interesting black and white photographs. However, Alastair Simpson, Managing Director of Airlife Publishing, persuaded me to have an all-colour production to show these colourful aircraft off at their best. I'm sure you won't be disappointed.

Photographs credited to A&AEE and RAE are Crown Copyright and reproduced by kind permission of A&AEE Public Relations Officer, Sqn. Ldr. John Taylor, and former RAE Public Relations Officers, Ken Meadows and David Horner.

Front Cover

(Top left:) Once used by Prince Charles for twin conversion pilot training, BEAGLE Basset CC.1, XS770, was later used by the ETPS and is seen alongside RAE Viscount, XT575, at Fairford in July 1985 during the International Air Tattoo. (Photo: Adrian Balch)

(Centre:) SEPECAT Jaguar ACT (Active Control Technology), XX765, displays its extended wing leading edges after the Farnborough Air Show in September 1985.
(Photo: Courtesy British Aerospace)

(Top right:) RAE Canberra B.6 (mods) in the static park at Boscombe Down during the TVS Air Show in June 1990. (Photo: Adrian Balch)

Rear Cover

(Top:) SEPECAT Jaguar T.2A, ZB615 of the RAE's Institute of Aviation Medicine taxies out at Fairford in July 1991, on completion of the International Air Tattoo. (Photo: Adrian Balch)

(Bottom:) RAE Vickers Viscount, XT661, in its original colour scheme at Abingdon in September 1978. (Photo: Adrian Balch)

Copyright © 1993 Adrian M. Balch

First published in the UK in 1993 by
Airlife Publishing Limited

British Library Cataloguing in Publication Data
A catalogue record for this book is
available from the British Library

ISBN 1 85310 349 7

Printed in Singapore by Kyodo Printing PTE Ltd.

Airlife Publishing Ltd.

101 Longden Road, Shrewsbury SY3 9EB, England

CONTENTS

Aircraft of the:

INTRODUCTION

For many years, the often highly colourful and heavily modified aircraft of the Ministry of Defence (Procurement Executive) have fascinated aviation enthusiasts through their elusive nature and clandestine operations. These aircraft often sprout 'lumps and bumps', radomes and probes, and their insides are frequently completely different from standard squadron aircraft. Tests and trials on military equipment are generally classified and it is for this reason that the fleet of aircraft seldom appears in public. It is only in recent years that these aircraft have started appearing at UK air shows thanks, mainly, to the work of the International Air Tattoo committee, who have formed a good relationship with MoD (PE) and have managed to bring some of their elusive machines to air shows at Greenham Common, Middle Wallop, Bournemouth-Hurn, and Fairford. Until then, the odd machine would appear in the static park of the RAF's Battle of Britain displays once a year, yet seldom elsewhere. Therefore, it has taken some twenty-plus years to accumulate the photographs in this book.

The period covered is 1960 onwards, as before 1960 few of these aircraft wore any special colour schemes or markings to denote that they were operated by the Establishments. As the object of this book is to illustrate interesting colour schemes and markings, 1960 seemed a convenient cut-off date, although full histories of each Establishment have been recorded. A large number of aircraft have been operated by MoD(PE) and its predecessors since 1960 and it is not possible to illustrate them all. It is hoped that your favourite aircraft are not omitted and that all the main colourful and interesting machines are included.

During the late 1960s and early '70s, the colour schemes became so varied that Boscombe Down began to repaint its aircraft in a standard colour scheme of white upper surfaces, light grey undersides with a red cheatline and fin. Likewise, most of the RAE aircraft adopted a similar scheme with blue trim instead of red. These schemes lasted until 1976, when the MoD(PE) decided to standardise on the smart red, white and dark blue scheme known as 'raspberry ripple'. The first aircraft to be painted were the Jaguar T.2s, XX915, and '916 of the ETPS and the scheme has spread throughout the fleet. The only aircraft that do not wear this scheme are those that are only on loan to MoD(PE) and those that require a different scheme for trials purposes.

THE PROCUREMENT EXECUTIVE

The Procurement Executive, part of the Ministry of Defence, is responsible for research, development, production and purchase of weapons systems and equipment for the Armed Forces, for the export promotion of defence equipment, and, on behalf of the Department of Industry, for certain civil aerospace research and development projects. It is the largest procurement task in the UK, dealing with about 4,500 companies, employing 50,000 people (not counting the Royal Ordnance Factories), and controls several research establishments. To meet the needs of flying-related systems, the PE operates a fleet of over 200 British military aircraft, scattered over several airfields in England, Scotland, Wales and Northern Ireland. Flying activities range from fundamental aerodynamic research, through type development to minor avionics assessment. Handling advice, limitations and operating data in aircrew manuals are based very largely on trials flown in the PE aircraft.

There are around forty types of aircraft (excluding marks) in the PE fleet at any one time, including representative aircraft of nearly all those in the three Services, plus many that are not. They currently range from the veteran Dakota at Farnborough to the newest prototypes such as the Tornado F.3, based at the type's factory at Warton. Up until recently, the most numerous type used by the PE was the Canberra, of which no less than 130 of all marks have been used for tests and trials over the years. The PE aircraft are divided between the Aircraft & Armament Evaluation Establishment (A&AEE) and the Empire Test Pilots School (ETPS) both at Boscombe Down, and the Royal Aerospace Establishment (RAE) at Farnborough and four out-stations.

On 1st April 1991, the four non-nuclear research establishments were extracted from MoD(PE) to form the Defence Research Agency: ARE, RAE, RARDE and RSRE. Porton stayed in Government control and A&AEE became part of the Directorate General of Test and Evaluation (DGT&E) in 1992, together with many of the Ranges which were previously in the ownership of the research establishments.

THE AIRCRAFT & ARMAMENT EVALUATION ESTABLISHMENT (A&AEE)

The history of the A&AEE can be traced back to the outbreak of World War I in 1914, when the experimental work of the Royal Flying Corps squadrons began to interrupt other flying activities of the CFS at Upavon, so an Experimental Flight was set up in December 1914. In April 1916, the title was changed to Test Flight, CFS, and the following month the armament work was hived off, with the Armament Experimental Flight moving to Orfordness on the Suffolk coast. The Aircraft Testing Flight remained at Upavon until 1917, being allocated Squadron status from December 1916. January 1917 saw a move to Martlesham Heath, occupying a newly-created airfield and hangars on heathland to the east of Ipswich.

At Martlesham, the title Aeroplane Experimental Station was adopted (Orfordness becoming the Armament Experimental Station). In April 1920, the title changed again, to Aeroplane Experimental Establishment, and between 1919 and 1921, the armament work was progressively taken on at Martlesham, Orfordness closing down in June 1921. The title of Aeroplane and Armament Experimental Establishment dated from 1924, by which time the performance testing unit had been given RAF squadron status as No.22 (from 1 May 1923); the armament testing aircraft were formed into No.13 Sqn (on 20 March 1924). These squadrons had provision to be equipped, in case of national emergency, with D.H.9As to operate in the day bombing role; they continued in this manner until 1934, when the two squadrons were 'moved' (on paper) to Donnibristle and Abingdon and reformed as operational units. In this period, the A&AEE steadily increased its skills in the scientific assessment of handling and performance of all British aeroplanes (including, until 1937, civil types, for which it acted as the airworthiness authority on behalf of the Air Ministry) and such foreign types as the Services had a special interest in. The thoroughness, and the independence, of testing by the A&AEE quickly become a byword.

The facilities at Martlesham Heath were adequate, but its geographical location could hardly have been worse in 1939, almost the nearest point on the English mainland to Germany. As war with Germany became inevitable, the A&AEE hastily prepared to move, and on 3 September 1939 its precious prototypes were flown out to Boscombe Down, together with the various supporting aircraft, key personnel and equipment.

At Boscombe Down – but a few air miles from Upavon where the unit had been born – the A&AEE redoubled its efforts to ensure that the Services received the aeroplanes they needed, in a condition in which they could safely be operated. The pace of activities and the size of the establishment doubled and doubled again as new operational needs developed. During World War II, the closely-guarded work of the A&AEE proved invaluable and contributed to the Allied victory.

Today, the A&AEE continues its work as the official centre for the acceptance testing of all military aircraft and associated equipment intended for use by the Services. Other Establishments of the MoD Procurement Executive are responsible for the research and development of many of the items which equip a modern aircraft, the Royal Aircraft Establishment for instance, being responsible for much fundamental research in aerodynamics, structures, aviation electronics (or avionics) and weapons, but at Boscombe Down the complete aircraft is evaluated against the requirements laid down for it. The requirement for a particular type of aircraft arises initially from a survey of the likely world situation some years ahead which is made by the appropriate staffs in the Ministry of Defence and associated departments. At the same time a review is made of state of the art aerodynamics, structures, engines, weapons and the like and an assessment is made of the feasibility of producing a particular type of aircraft. Once that has been done, the MoD Procurement Executive produces a specification based on the Staff Requirement and the aviation industry is then invited to produce an aircraft to meet the specification; Boscombe Down gets involved even at this early stage by offering advice based on experience with similar types of aircraft. Acting as the buying agent for the Ministry of Defence, the Procurement Executive instructs the manufacturer to build the aircraft. The Establishment then flies the aircraft, calls for its modification (if necessary), defines operational limitations (as necessary) and specifies special training for Service personnel (if required); such a sequence applies equally to the introduction of special equipment and armament as to the introduction of a brand new aircraft, or of new marks. Once all the stringent flight and ground trials have met the specifications, the aircraft is then recommended for CA (Controller Aircraft) release. Until such a release is given, an aircraft cannot be flown by Service pilots in the normal line of duty.

In 1992, A&AEE changed its title from the Aeroplane & Armament Experimental Establishment to the Aircraft & Armament Evaluation Establishment, conveniently keeping the same initials. Under a civilian Chief Superintendent, trials are currently divided among four Assessment Divisions: Armament Systems Division; Engineering Systems Division; Mission Systems Division and Aircraft Dynamics Division. Until 1988,

Blackburn Beverley C.1 XB261 of A&AEE Boscombe Down emerges from a stormy sky over the Wiltshire countryside on 14 August 1970 and is illuminated by a shaft of sunlight. (Photo: Adrian Balch).

the flying tasks were organised through the Flying Division, which was divided up into 'A', 'B' and 'D' Squadrons plus the Empire Test Pilots School. Today, Flying Division contains two squadrons which carry out all of the flying for the assessment divisions and is divided according to the type and role of the aircraft. Since January 1988 all fixed wing aircraft are flown by the Fixed Wing Test Squadron which also operates photographic chase and support aircraft. Rotary Wing Test Squadron is concerned with all helicopters irrespective of the Service user. Both Squadrons operate laboratory aircraft for the Navigation and Radio Division.

Also at A&AEE, but as a lodger unit, is Handling Squadron, not concerned with acceptance testing, but responsible for writing the Pilot's Notes and other handbooks forming the 'bibles' for Service use of the aircraft equipment in question.

Each division is divided into seven divisions, each headed by a Group Captain or civilian equivalent. An Air Commodore is overall head of the Establishment and the Chief Superintendent, a civilian, is responsible for the trials divisions.

Administration Division headed by the Secretary, interprets policy locally and provides the administrative backing for all of the other divisions, operating mainly in the field of provisioning, personnel and finance. It includes security, transport, stores, typing and printing, telecommunications, training and accommodation. It also liaises with the Defence Works Services (DWS).

Technical Services Division has the task of maintaining all aircraft of the A&AEE fleet and the servicing of all airborne electrical and instrument equipment. Photographic facilities and the Apprentice Training School are included in this division, weapon servicing and the maintenance of airfield services is also the responsibility of this division.

(Right:) Armstrong-Whitworth Argosy C.1, XN817, served all its life with A&AEE Boscombe Down since delivery on 24 July 1961. It wore the standard RAF Argosy colour scheme of white and silver with blue cheatline plus the addition of black/white checks on the rear doors for photographic purposes during parachute extraction trials. In 1972 the fins were repainted red, and light grey replaced the aluminium areas by 1974, with red trim being added to the wingtips and spinners, as shown here on 30 April 1974. XN817 had the distinction of being the last Argosy in military service. On the point of retirement it suffered a premature withdrawal, when an undercarriage leg collapsed on landing at RAE West Freugh on 1 October 1984.

The Empire Test Pilots' School also operated Argosy, XR105, in a near identical colour scheme from 26 April 1971 until it crashed at Boscombe Down on 27 April 1976, killing all on board. (Photo: Adrian Balch)

(Right:) Blackburn Beverley C.1, XB261, was first flown from Brough, Yorkshire on 5 July 1955. It never saw service with the RAF, spending its entire life with the A&AEE at Boscombe Down on a variety of tasks and trials. Its main duties with the A&AEE involved flying as a stable and large-capacity parachute platform. During 1966/7, it was used to develop the lo-drop system of supplying troops, using a low-flying aircraft. This developed into the ULLA system (Ultra Low Level Air-drop). This was a system of dropping palletised loads (including Land-Rovers and field guns) from an aircraft flying at low level, by streaming a number of parachutes out from the rear of the aircraft and pulling the load out of the hold. XB261 had a band of red dayglo strips round the nose, rear fuselage and wingtips. A red cheatline divided the white room from a natural metal airframe; spinners were matt black. This was the penultimate Beverley to be retired, making its last flight on 6 October 1971 from Boscombe Down to Southend for preservation. It lasted for nearly twenty years exposed to the elements, but eventually had to be scrapped due to corrosion. XB261 is seen here at Biggin Hill in September 1968 during the annual Battle of Britain air show. (Photo: Author's collection)

(Below:) Bristol 170 Freighter Mk.31C, XJ470 (c/n 13217) spent all its life with A&AEE at Boscombe Down, being delivered there on 21 February 1955. It was retired from service in July 1968 and flown to Lasham in January 1969 for intended sale to Midland Air Cargo, but the deal fell through and the aircraft was broken up at Lasham during 1969. Wearing orange dayglo trim, XJ470 was used to transport spares and equipment around Europe and is seen here at Woodford, during a visit to Hawker Siddeley Aviation on 7 July 1967. (Photo: Iain MacPherson)

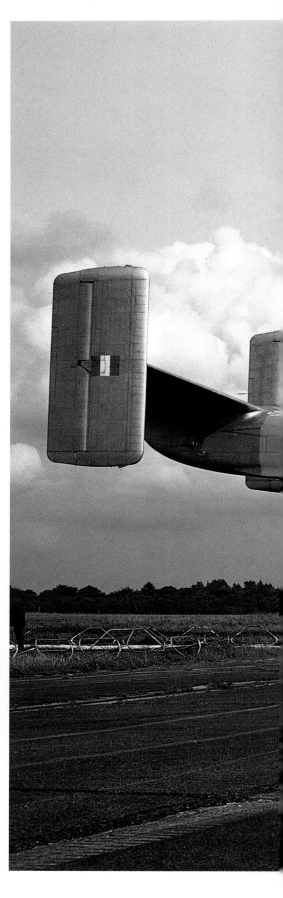

(Right:) Bristol Britannia Srs. 312F, XX367 (c/n 13421) first flew on 9 April 1958 and was delivered to BOAC on 20 May 1958, registered G-AOVM. It was transferred to British Eagle International Airlines on 28 March 1964, named 'Team Spirit'. It was converted to 312F cargo status in December 1967 and sold to Air Spain, being registered EC-BSY on 1 December 1969. It was a regular visitor to Gatwick on charter flights until it was sold to MoD(PE) in November 1971. It was transferred to A&AEE Boscombe Down on 3 May 1972 becoming XX367 and was used on general transport duties until late 1983, when it was withdrawn from use and stored. It was sold to Katale Air Transport of Zaire in March 1984, then to Business Cash Flow Aviation in April 1989, becoming the last airworthy Britannia worldwide, until its withdrawal from service in 1991.

XX367 wore an overall light grey finish with white roof, red fin, wingtips and cheatline. It continued to carry the name, 'Team Spirit', from its British Eagle days. It is seen here during its last flight in military service, when it was ferried from A&AEE Boscombe Down to Cranfield on 24th February 1984. This dramatic close-up air-to-air shot was taken by the late Stephen Piercy from a Piper Seneca.

(Below:) Short Belfast C.1, XR366, was the only one of its type to adopt non-standard markings, when it was on loan to A&AEE Boscombe Down during 1965/6. It was used for winterisation trials and was given arctic red trim to make it conspicuous in the snow at Churchill and other bases in north Canada. It was also named 'Eskimo Belle' and was given a Canadian flag on the nose. On completion of trials, XR366 went to Marshalls of Cambridge for repainting, where it was photographed in April 1968. Afterwards, it joined the rest of the Belfast fleet with 53 Squadron at Brize Norton until it was retired and scrapped on 8 August 1979. (Photo: R. G. Griggs)

Performance and Trials Management Division is responsible for the planning, control and co-ordination of the Establishment's effort. It is also responsible for the handling and performance assessments of all fixed and rotary wing aircraft and for providing recommendations on operating limitations. Support is given to the specialist divisions in providing a computer service, and the Division is also responsible for the development of test instrumentation used in flight trials.

Engineering Division conducts tests to assess the safety, efficiency and reliability of all systems in an aircraft apart from those specific to armament, navigation and photography. It specialises in the performance of hydraulic, fuel, electrical and air conditioning systems and is responsible for

operating many of the Establishment's test facilities. The division is also responsible for the development and clearance of para-trooping and supply-dropping methods and equipment.

Armament Division is concerned with the safe and reliable carriage and release of weapons from aircraft. It carries out assessments of the complete weapons installation, the integrity of the weapons carriage in flight and the safe release and satisfactory functioning of the weapon in the target area.

Navigation and Radio Division conducts acceptance trials of navigation/attack equipment and all radio/radar installations in new military aircraft and of new equipment fitted to existing aircraft. It is also

concerned with systems considered for installation in the future and the evaluation of selected civil navigation systems.

Flying Division contains two squadrons which carry out all of the flying for the assessment divisions and is divided according to the type and role of the aircraft. Since January 1988 all fixed wing aircraft are flown by the Fixed Wing Test Squadron which also operates photographic chase and support aircraft. Rotary Wing Test Squadron is concerned with all helicopters irrespective of the Service user. Both Squadrons operate laboratory aircraft for the Navigation and Radio Division. In May 1992, the A&AEE changed its title to Aircraft & Armament *Evaluation* Establishment.

(Right:) Blackburn Buccaneer S.2, XN974, was the first production S.Mk.2 and spent all its life with A&AEE Boscombe Down, thus retaining its original dark grey and white Fleet Air Arm colour scheme. XN974 first flew on 6 June 1964 and immediately began trials with A&AEE, including 'tropical' trials in the USA during 1965. These culminated in a non-stop flight from Goose Bay, Canada, to Lossiemouth without refuelling – a total of 1,950 miles. Afterwards, it went to 'C' Squadron of the A&AEE, the RN Test Squadron, for weapons development until May 1971 when the squadron disbanded. It then returned to British Aerospace at Warton. Its status and future are unknown. On the fin, it wore the badge of the RN Test Squadron, which was applied in late 1970. XN974 is seen here on finals on a fine summer's day in July 1970.

(Below:) The A&AEE's Royal Naval Test Squadron's badge on the tail of XN974 in March 1971. (Photos: Adrian Balch)

XK527 was one of the Buccaneer Development Batch aircraft that took part in carrier trials on HMS Ark Royal during 1961. In 1963, it was converted to an S.Mk.2 prototype, together with XK526, at Brough. In 1965 it was involved in 'tropical' trials in the USA, after which it went to the A&AEE's 'C' Squadron for missile development and was used for Martel trials during 1970-74, during which it retained its naval colour scheme of overall extra dark sea grey and white serials, with the addition of a white Martel silhouette marking on the nose. XK527 was fitted with a long instrumentation nose probe throughout its life, which culminated in it being withdrawn from use at Holme-on-Spalding Moor in the late '80s. It was broken up and only its nose survives with a private collection at New Milton, Hants. It is seen here on finals during Martel Missile trials in July 1970. (Photo: Adrian Balch)

Blackburn Buccaneer S.2B, XW988, was one of a trio specially built for the RAE at West Freugh which were delivered during May 1974. They have been used in weapons trials and are fitted with special underwing camera pylons for photographing the dropping trials. This unusual colour scheme of yellow, dark green and white was specially developed as being most suitable for the kinethodolite work involved in such trials. These three aircraft were initially flown devoid of national markings, but later had Type 'B' roundels added above the wings and a swept red and blue fin flash. The serials are in white on the rear fuselage and black on the bomb-day door, which is really unusual. This came about by accident, as when the colour scheme had been drawn out, someone had scrawled the serial number across the drawing. This was intended to show the paint shop which drawing applied to which airframe. However, the scrawl happened to have been written across the bomb-bay on the drawing and was faithfully reproduced by the painters on the real aircraft. All three aircraft were thus painted. Since then, XW986 and '987 have been repainted in the 'raspberry ripple' scheme, leaving XW988 still in the original scheme at the time of writing. It is seen here visiting Lyneham on 30 June 1990, for the Station Families Day. (Photo: Adrian Balch)

(Bottom:) WH876 was one of several Canberra B.2s assigned to the A&AEE's Bomber & Maritime Flight Test/B Squadron. It was converted to a U.14 drone aircraft and first flew as such on 10 August 1961. It was converted back to a B.2, and painted in an overall white scheme with pale blue trim as seen here at Chivenor on 4 August 1972. (Photo: Dave Cross). (see photo on page 20)

(Below:) English Electric Canberra B(1)6, WT309, was one of the last testbeds in service with the A&AEE, and has seen service since February 1958. It is shown here at the International Air Tattoo at Fairford on 11 July 1985. It was grounded in 1988 and is currently used by the A&AEE Apprentice School. (Photo: Adrian Balch)

(Right:) This flying shot of A&AEE Canberra B(1)6, WT309, shows the underside markings off to advantage, especially the unusual white bomb-bay doors, as it climbs out of Fairford on 15 July 1985. (Photo: Adrian Balch)

(Below:) During 1963, a feasibility study into the artificial propagation of aircraft icing conditions was initiated, and contracts were placed jointly with the English Electric Co. and Flight Refuelling Ltd for design and development of an icing tanker aircraft. This emerged as Canberra WV787, delivered to Boscombe Down early in 1967, a hybrid Mk.2/8 aircraft, extensively modified to provide an airborne water spray system which could provide localised calibrated icing cloud conditions comparable with natural phenomena. A 600-gallon stainless steel tank was fitted in the bomb bay, and one of the fuselage fuel tanks was isolated from the fuel system and converted to carry 300 gallons of water. A hydraulic pump in the bomb bay drew water from the tank and delivered it via an external boom to a 22-nozzle spray rake mounted behind the fuselage tail cone. Compressed air was bled from the engines to the rake, where water and air mixed to provide a freely atomised water spray. Natural expansion in flight provided a cloud of up to 90 sq.ft at sixty gallons per minute at 200ft range. The spray system was controlled from the observer's position. Icing tests were successfully carried out on many aircraft types, the most famous of which was Concorde.

Before becoming an icing tanker, WV787 was operated by Ferranti, with whom it had a B(I)8 nose and Buccaneer nose radome to develop that type's 'Blue Parrot' radar.

Painted gloss black overall, the nose cone was initially unpainted brown fibreglass, but was later overpainted gloss black. All lettering was in white and for a while the A&AEE badge appeared on the fin in a yellow disc. After an active life, WV787 was retired to Abingdon in August 1984 for battle damage repair training but was rescued in October 1985 and transferred to the Newark Air Museum, where it resides today. The photograph shows WV787 spraying water from its rig during a sortie from Boscombe Down in 1981. (A&AEE photo)

(Below left:) During 1980-88, WH876 replaced WJ638 as an ejection-seat test vehicle with A&AEE and was painted in this striking black and white checked scheme with red trim. It was withdrawn from use in December 1988 and stored at Boscombe Down until January 1990, when it was scrapped. WH876 is seen landing at Greenham Common for the International Air Tattoo on 22 July 1983. (Photo: Adrian Balch)

(Below:) Shorts-built Canberra B.2,WJ638, was used by the A&AEE for ejection-seat trials until being struck off charge in 1978. Originally built as a B.2,WJ638 was later modified as a U.10 radio-controlled drone. On its arrival at Boscombe Down in March 1964, the radio-control equipment and all furnishings of the navigator's compartment behind the pilot were stripped out. A thick bulkhead was mounted at the rear of this compartment and a light internal skin fitted to fair off the other surfaces as ejection sorties were made with the rear hatch removed. The rear bulkhead served as a mount for the test seats and two could be mounted side by side for individual or almost simultaneous ejection. Two 16mm cine cameras were installed in each wing, angled to record the emergence of the seat and to follow its trajectory for a short distance, another being mounted ahead of the fin looking forward and a sixth in the tail cone looking astern. Others were inside the ejection compartment.

Many ejections were made from this aircraft, using all types of seats with dummies, flight trials normally taking place at 500ft over the Larkhill Ranges. The speed range of the Canberra for these trials was 130-450kts. Ground level ejections at 90-100kts could also be made. WJ638 was painted white overall with orange-strip dayglo trim. The A&AEE badge appeared on the fin on a yellow disc and the number of ejections made were marked by rows of small dayglo triangles on the nose. WJ638 served in this role until it was withdrawn from use and transported to the fire dump at Predannack on 5 January 1978. It is seen here on finals during its heyday in June 1970. (Photo: Adrian Balch).

(Left:) A&AEE Gloster Javelin FAW.2, XA778, in its startling all-dayglo orange finish, during one of its rare public appearances, at Coltishall in September 1967 for the annual Battle of Britain display. More information and an underside view of this aircraft appears on page 27. (Photo: Author's collection)

(Below:) Nose details on the last airworthy Comet in the world, the A&AEE's Mk.4C, XS235, showing the name 'Canopus' and a badge applied in 1988 to mark the aircraft's 25th birthday, 1963-1988. (Photo: Adrian Balch)

De Havilland Comet 4C, XS235, has served all its life with A&AEE at Boscombe Down as a flying laboratory and is the last airworthy Comet in the world. XS235 first flew from Chester on 26 September 1963 to Hatfield. After fitting out with racks and interior fittings, it was delivered to Boscombe Down on 2 December. Painted white and grey, the red cheatline is thinly outlined in dark blue. The fin was painted red in early 1971 and the aircraft carries the name 'Canopus' on the nose. Apart from the addition of the red fin, the colour scheme has remained unchanged since delivery and the aircraft has resisted adopting the 'raspberry ripple' colour scheme at the time of writing. These photographs show Comet 4C, XS235, near Boscombe Down on 29 July 1992 and were specially taken for this book. (Photos: Adrian Balch)

(Below:) For many years, the A&AEE at Boscombe Down has employed three all-yellow North American Harvards as photo-chase aircraft, having continued in service after World War II. FT375, KF183 and KF314 were a familiar trio until the latter crashed and was written-off on 22 February 1982, near Boscombe Down. All three A&AEE Harvards are seen here at Bassingbourn, Cambs. on 27 May 1978, as part of the Harvard's fortieth Anniversary celebrations. (Photo: Adrian Balch)

(Right:) FT375 is one of the pair of surviving Harvards operated by A&AEE and is seen here near Boscombe Down in 1981. (A&AEE photo)

(Below:) Gloster Javelin FAW.9, XH897, served with Nos 25 33 and 5 Squadrons before going to Bristol Siddeley Engines for test work at Filton from 20 July 1965. It then moved to the A&AEE at Boscombe Down on 1 April 1968 to replace Javelin FAW.2, XA778. It retained its camouflage until at least June 1968 when it gained its superb red and white colour scheme, which reflected the aircraft's role as a calibration checker for other aircraft's instruments and as a pacer aircraft. Upon retirement it was replaced by a Phantom and was acquired by the Imperial War Museum and flown to Duxford on 24 January 1975 for static display, where it resides today. (Photos: A&AEE)

(Right:) Gloster Javelin FAW.2, XA778, was a calibrated test vehicle with an F(AW)7 engine installation and with an F(AW)8 flying control system. Painted orange dayglo overall, it arrived at Boscombe Down on 1 March 1961 and was used as a pacer aircraft at A&AEE to determine Air Speed Indicator (ASI) pressure error correction on other aircraft. The photograph shows the underside colours and markings to advantage, including the flaps strangely painted in black/yellow target-tug stripes, when depicted on 27 July 1967. XA778 was withdrawn from use and struck off charge on 28 March 1969, when it was replaced by Javelin FAW.9, XH897. (Photo: Adrian Balch)

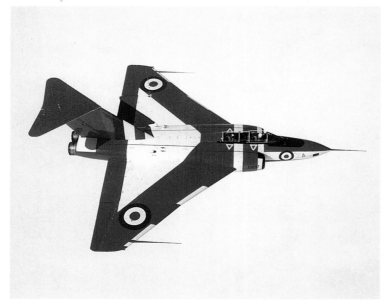

(Left:) Pilatus Britten-Norman BN.2T Islander, ZF573, is a one-off type operating with A&AEE for Sea Spray missile trials. Based at Bembridge, it is currently owned by MoD(PE) and wears military colours and markings and was previously registered G-SRAY. It is seen here at Middle Wallop on 18 July 1988. (Photo: Adrian Balch)

(Below:) One of the few surviving airworthy Meteors is WL419, which is a hybrid T.7 used for ejection seat trials by Martin-Baker Ltd at Chalgrove, Oxon. For extra stability it has been fitted with a tail unit from a Meteor F.8, making it a T.7½. After RAF service, WL419 was transferred to the Ministry of Aviation in August 1963 for use by Martin-Baker. It was put into storage at Chalgrove until being made airworthy again in 1979. Test ejections are made from the open rear cockpit, the aircraft operating from Chalgrove and from Boscombe Down over the Larkhill Ranges in conjunction with A&AEE. The photograph shows WL419 between sorties at Chalgrove on 27 February 1986. (Photo: Adrian Balch)

(Right:) De Havilland Sea Vixen FAW.1, XJ481, was one of a trio used by the Royal Navy Test Squadron of A&AEE for Martel Missile trials. XJ481 first flew on 2 September 1958 and was to enter a long career of test work. It was delivered to the Handling Squadron of the A&AEE at Boscombe Down on 28 November 1958. It was detached to HMS Centaur for trials during 1959, then shipped to Australia on 13 March 1960 for use with the Long Range Weapons Establishment at Woomera on weapons trials. It stayed in the desert until March 1967 when it came home by ship. It arrived in June and joined Hawker Siddeley Dynamics at Hatfield. It was back with the A&AEE for further trials on 6 November 1968 and served with 'C' Squadron on missile trials, ending with the Martel. A camera was fitted in the normally-pointed nose to film the trials. During this period it was painted in an unusual black and white colour scheme for calibrating duties, with roundels on the black portions only. It was retired and despatched to Yeovilton in March 1974 for the Fleet Air Arm Museum. However, as XJ481 had been heavily modified, including the flattened camera nose, it was not thought to be representative of the Sea Vixen family, so was withdrawn in 1985 and sold to a buyer in the USA. However, XJ481 never left the country and is currently at RNAY Fleetlands Museum. The photograph shows Sea Vixen FAW.1, XJ481, during Martel Missile trials in July 1972. (Photo: Adrian Balch)

(Below:) A fourth Piper PA-31 Navajo-Chieftain 350 operated by MoD(PE) is ZF622 which has been with the A&AEE at Boscombe Down since 1985. This aircraft, has, so far, resisted the 'raspberry ripple' colour scheme and retains its basic Piper company colours of tan brown overall with white and two-tone brown trim, upon which military markings have been applied. The photograph shows ZF622 on a visit to Lyneham on 19 May 1988. (Photo: Adrian Balch)

McDonnell Phantom FG.1, XT597, is the third pre-production F-4K for the Royal Navy and has served all its life with A&AEE at Boscombe Down, initially with the Royal Naval Test Squadron after delivery in 1968. It started life in the standard dark grey and white Fleet Air Arm colour scheme, which by 1977 had the fin and wingtips repainted red. XT597 was repainted in the 'raspberry ripple' scheme in time for the International Air Tattoo in July 1983, where the paint scheme was used as the backdrop for a lot of stickers to celebrate the Phantom's 25th Anniversary. The photograph shows XT597 arriving at Greenham Common on 20 July 1983, prior to the temporary anniversary markings being applied. (Photo: Adrian Balch)

Another shot of A&AEE Boscombe Down's Phantom FG.1,XT597, taken two years later, now with fin flash added. This photograph was taken at Fairford on 12 July 1985, during the International Air Tattoo. (Photo: Adrian Balch)

(Left:) Another Sea Vixen FAW.1 used in the Martel Missile programme by the A&AEE's Royal Naval Test Squadron was XJ488, painted black overall with a white lightning flash. It was delivered to A&AEE on 18 October 1967, adopting this colour scheme the following year. It was struck-off-charge on 6 December 1972 and burnt on the dump at Boscombe Down. The photograph shows XJ488 on finals in June 1970. (Photo: Adrian Balch)

(Below:) Hawker Hunter F.6, XE601, has been progressively modified up to FGA.9 standard, but has never been officially designated as such. It has been used jointly by the A&AEE and ETPS at Boscombe Down for many years, and is current at the time of writing. Painted in a smart grey and red scheme, XE601 has been used on a variety of trials. The photograph shows XE601 during gunnery trials on the Holbeach Range on 14 October 1974. (Photo: Adrian Balch)

(Bottom:) The same aircraft now repainted in the 'raspberry ripple' colour scheme seen at Boscombe Down during Air Tournament 92. (Photo: Adrian Balch)

(Below:) Handley Page Hastings C.1A, TG500, catches a glimmer of sunlight during the otherwise very wet A&AEE 50th Anniversary celebrations at Boscombe Down on 18 March 1971. The following year, this aircraft was retired and scrapped at Bicester. (Photo: Adrian Balch)

(Bottom:) During the '60s, the A&AEE's Royal Naval Test Section operated the two surviving examples of the Boulton-Paul Sea Balliol T.21, WP333 and WL732. The former was scrapped at Boscombe Down in July 1966, but WL732 survived and is currently preserved by the Cosford Aerospace Museum. It made its last flight to Coltishall, then to Henlow on 7 February 1969 and is depicted there on 25 May 1970, still in its final A&AEE silver and dayglo scheme. (Photo: Jeff Peck)

(Right:) During the '60s, the A&AEE operated a trio of Handley Page Hastings, TG500, TG502 and WD496. All three were white and natural metal with red dayglo trim. In 1971, they were repainted with the metal areas painted light grey and the dayglo red trim replaced by roundel-red paint. TG500 and TG502 had an Argosy-type thimble nose radome, while C.2 WD496 sported a nose probe and is seen here in June 1972, prior to being struck off charge and scrapped in 1973. (Photo: via Flt Lt John Hilliard)

THE EMPIRE TEST PILOTS' SCHOOL

The Empire Test Pilots' School was formed at Boscombe Down in 1943 with terms of reference 'to provide suitably trained pilots for test flying duties in aeronautical research and development establishments within the Service and the Industry'. For several years the School was the only institution of its kind in the world. Shortage of space at Boscombe Down caused a move to Cranfield in 1945. A further move in 1947 to Farnborough started a long and fruitful association with the Royal Aircraft Establishment. During twenty years at Farnborough, the School syllabus evolved progressively without major innovation until the setting up in 1963 of the Rotary Wing Course to meet a growing need for trained helicopter test pilots. In 1968 the School returned to the more open skies of Boscombe Down, where it renewed a close and valuable association with the Aeroplane and Armament Experimental Establishment. The Flight Test Engineer Course was added in 1974.

The Empire Test Pilots' School trains pilots and engineers for exacting roles in flight test teams concerned with the research, development and acceptance of Service aircraft and weapons systems.

The increasing complexity and expense of modern multi-mission aircraft and their associated equipment places increasing responsibility on those tasked with their safe and efficient development for the Armed Services. The extent and importance of the tasks demand the highest possible professional standards from test pilots and flight test engineers and the greatest possible understanding and co-operation between these key members of trials teams. The Empire Test Pilots' School aims to meet these requirements by teaching high-calibre operational pilots the demanding skills of the test pilot and by providing pilot and flight test engineer students with the opportunity of working closely together on challenging flight test exercises. To date, well over 1,000 pilots and engineers have graduated from the School, including nearly 500 from overseas.

Fixed and rotary courses are run concurrently from January to December each year and comprise officer pilots of the Royal Navy, the Army and the Royal Air Force and student flight test engineers selected from professional Ministry of Defence Procurement Executive staff. Military officers from Commonwealth and allied nations as well as civilians sponsored by foreign governments are also eligible. A typical

(Right:) 'Raspberry Ripple' Rotors – Seen under the tail boom of the Empire Test Pilots' School's Lynx is their Gazelle HT.3, XZ936, at Fairford during the International Air Tattoo on 22 July 1989. This is the only Gazelle to wear the MoD(PE) colour scheme. (Photo: Adrian Balch)

(Below:) Andover C.1, XS606, was initially delivered to the Andover OCU at Abingdon on 2 November 1966 in two-tone brown camouflage with black undersides. It then went to 52 Squadron at Seletar, Singapore on 23 November 1966 until that Squadron disbanded on 31 December 1969. It returned to Abingdon on 15 January 1970 to serve with 46 Squadron. After a short period at Thorney Island, XS606 was sent to 5MU at Kemble for storage on 17 December 1970. It was loaned to the Ministry of Defence (Procurement Executive) on 3 August 1972, being taken out of storage and delivered to RAE

Farnborough on 7 December of that year. It was repainted in the colour scheme shown here, apart from 'Royal Aircraft Establishment' titles and a white rear fuselage. During the summer of 1973 it was used for parachute extraction trials and general transport duties by the RAE at Farnborough and Bedford. On 1 August 1975, XS606 was transferred to the Empire Test Pilots' School at Boscombe Down, with the titles being changed as shown here during a visit to East Midlands Airport in March 1976. (Photo: Author's collection)

(Right:) BAC One-Eleven 479FU, ZE432 (c/n 250), was initially delivered to the Fijian airline, Air Pacific, on 4 August 1973. The MoD purchased it in March 1984 for use by the Empire Test Pilots' School at Boscombe Down, its registration changing from DQ-FBV to ZE432. The aircraft is currently with ETPS and is seen here at the International Air Tattoo, Fairford on 23 July 1989. (Photo: Adrian Balch)

course consists of nineteen students of nine different nationalities. The intensive course work is broken up into three terms.

The first term begins with three weeks' ground instruction aimed at bringing students of diverse academic ability and background to an adequate standard in mathematics, mechanics, aerodynamics and other basic subjects before instruction in the theoretical background to test flying begins. Ground school follows, where students learn the theory of aircraft stability, control and performance, as well as methods of performance analysis and reduction. Also a course in avionics systems is taught, the whole ground school syllabus being carefully phased to match the practical flying exercises.

At the completion of the preliminary ground school phase, students begin appropriate conversion and familiarisation flying on the eight fixed wing and four rotary wing types which normally make up the school fleet. The composition of the fleet is chosen to reflect types and classes of aircraft in operational service. In 1987, the school gained an ADV Tornado and in 1988 an advanced replacement for the Varistab Basset in the shape of a specially modified Hawk jet – the 'ASTRA' Hawk – was added to the fleet. The rotary wing inventory was boosted by the arrival of a new Lynx Mk.7 in 1988, and in 1989 Sea King Mk.4 ZG829 replaced XV370.

For the test flying exercises the courses are divided into a number of syndicates, each under the direction of a test flying tutor. The tutors, who are all experienced graduates of recognised test pilot school with at least three years' experience of flight test flying, reinforce the classroom exercise brief with a detailed syndicate brief and fly with each student for the demonstration and practice of test techniques. Exercise flights are then carried out by the test pilot students, with flight test engineer students providing the planning and organisation of the flight. The students fly some 150 hours during the eleven month course. The early handling and performance exercises are designed to be straightforward in theory and execution, but, as students gain experience, exercises become progressively more demanding of technical expertise and flying skill.

During the first term all students are introduced to the variable stability Basset. This aircraft, which joined the school fleet in 1973, simulated a wide variety of stability and control characteristics using an analogue computer and autopilot actuators. The Basset is an invaluable tool for demonstrating the theory taught in the ground school without the constraints of the relatively conventional handling qualities of other aircraft in the School fleet. In the second term, handling qualities are taught and performance exercises carried out.

Also, both rotary and fixed wing students carry out a practical assessment of typical airborne navigation/attack systems, including navigation, weapon aiming and night vision systems.

The third term commences with advanced stability and control exercises, starting with a single flight assessment of an unfamiliar aircraft type, progressing to the most demanding exercise of the course: the Preview. Hard work and dedication are the keys to successful completion of the ETPS course. However, the rewards are great and graduates can rightfully expect to continue to be involved in the world's most stimulating and absorbing aerospace projects.

As regards colour schemes of ETPS aircraft, until the 'raspberry ripple' scheme was introduced in 1976, most aircraft wore standard operational colour schemes with the addition of a large number code on the fuselage. Apart from the Viscounts, the first ETPS aircraft to get their own colour scheme were the Hunters, which adopted an overall reddish-orange colour with white and black trim during the early '60s. Around 1970, this was changed to light grey with red trim, while Scout XP165 was painted in a smart red and white scheme. However, before the fleet looked too motley, the 'raspberry ripple' scheme was introduced and today the whole ETPS fleet is resplendent in this scheme.

(Left:) H.S. Andover C.1, XS606, of the ETPS, taken in September 1987, on approach shows the position of the underwing markings to advantage. Also worthy of note is the non-standard instrumentation nose probe. At the time of writing, XS606 was still in current use as a multi-engine trainer for test pilots and for general transport duties. (Photo: Adrian Balch)

(Below:) By June 1977, XS606 had adopted a red fin and this was followed by a complete repaint to the 'raspberry ripple' scheme as shown here during a visit to Bournemouth-Hurn Airport on 17 August 1984. (Photo: Adrian Balch)

EMPIRE TEST PILOTS SCHOOL

(Left:) BEAGLE Basset CC.1,XS743, was the second production Basset and the first completed at Rearsby. It has spent all its life at Boscombe Down, initially on trials with A&AEE during 1965, then with the Empire Test Pilots' School since 20 December 1967, with a brief period at Farnborough. It was loaned to the Cranfield Institute of Technology during 1971/2 for gust research, then returned to Boscombe Down joining three other Bassets with ETPS, XS742, XS765 and the ex-'Reagle Beagle', XS770, XS742, '743 and '765 shared the colour scheme shown here for many years, the red fin and cheatline being worn from 1973 until their retirement. XS743 is seen here on finals in September 1987. (Photo: Adrian Balch)

(Below:) Of the Basset quartet used by the ETPS, only XS743 survived to see the smart 'raspberry ripple' scheme and was the last Basset in service. It is seen here at Boscombe Down on 12 June 1992 during Air Tournament 92. (Photo: Adrian Balch)

(Right:) The Empire Test Pilots' School currently operates three BAe Hawk T.1s from Boscombe Down. All three are seen here with their Hunter T.7 and Jet Provost T.5 in July 1992 during Air Tournament '92 at their home base. (Photo: Adrian Balch)

(Below:) SEPECAT Jaguar T.2A, XX830, is one of a pair used by the Empire Test Pilots' School at Boscombe Down, the other being XX145. This pair replaced the original ETPS Jaguar T.2s, XX915 and XX916 which were written-off on 17 January 1984 and 24 July 1981 respectively. Painted in the smart 'raspberry ripple' scheme, XX830 is seen here taxying at Fairford on 24 July 1989, after participating in the International Air Tattoo. (Photo: Adrian Balch)

(Bottom:) The first production Jet Provost T.5, XS230, has been operated by the Empire Test Pilots' School for all its life and is with them today. Originally delivered in a grey and dayglo scheme, it is seen here at Boscombe Down in 1976 wearing its interim red, white and grey livery prior to being painted in the current 'raspberry ripple' scheme. (Photo: Author's collection)

(Below:) Westland Lynx AH.7, ZD560, currently flies with the Empire Test Pilots' School from Boscombe Down. It joined the ETPS in 1988 and operates alongside five other rotary types in the fleet. It is seen here at Fairford on 20 July 1989. (Photo: Adrian Balch)

(Below:) Westland Sea King HC.4, ZG829, of the Empire Test Pilots' School on standby fire-fighting duties at Boscombe Down during The International Air Tattoo in June 1990. Unfortunately, this machine crashed and caught fire itself in October 1992 and has possibly been written-off. (Photo: Adrian Balch)

(Right:) The surviving Hunter T.7 with the Empire Test Pilots' School is XL564, which has adopted the 'raspberry ripple' colour scheme. It has spent all its life at Boscombe Down, being delivered there on 10 March 1960. It was used for UHF radio trials the following year and was transferred to the ETPS in 1983, with whom it is current. The photograph shows XL564 landing at Fairford on 21 July 1989, for the International Air Tattoo. (Photo: Adrian Balch)

(Bottom:) Hawker Hunter T.7, XL579, was delivered to No.229 OCU on 29 July 1958 and was transferred to the Empire Test Pilots' School at Farnborough in 1965. It was painted in the red, white and black ETPS scheme until the school moved to Boscombe Down in 1968, when it was repainted light grey and red. XL579 was in service until the mid-70s, when it was withdrawn from use and scrapped. The photograph shows XL579 in its original ETPS colour scheme at Coltishall on 17 September 1966. (Photo: John Hughes)

(Below:) Another Hunter T.7 operated by the Empire Test Pilots School was XL616, which served until 18 May 1976, when it was refurbished and transferred to TWU/45 Squadron at Wittering. It went on to serve with 2 TWU at Lossiemouth and was withdrawn from use at the end of 1991, being put into storage at Shawbury. The photograph shows XL616 in its final ETPS grey and red scheme at Boscombe Down on 18 March 1971. (Photo: Adrian Balch)

(Below:) Scottish Aviation Twin Pioneer Srs.3, XT610, was originally the Scottish Aviation demonstrator, G-APRS, until it was delivered to the Empire Test Pilots' School at Farnborough in 1965. It flew in a white, silver and dark blue scheme coded '22' until 1973, when it was repainted white, grey and red. It was withdrawn from use on 1 February 1975 and sold to Flight One Ltd at Staverton, becoming G-BCWF. In 1992, it was sold to the National Environment Research Council and operated by Air Atlantique, from Coventry, remaining one of the last of its type in airworthy condition. The photograph shows XT610 on finals to Greenham Common on 6 July 1973 for the Embassy Air Tattoo. (Photo: Adrian Balch)

(Below:) Vickers V.745D Viscount, XR802 (c/n 198) was one of a pair operated by the Empire Test Pilots' School, initially at Farnborough from April 1962 transferring to Boscombe Down in 1968. It first flew on 24 September 1956 as N7442, being delivered to Capital Airlines, which merged into United Airlines on 1 June 1961. It was leased to Northeast Airlines from 21 June to 25 September 1961, then was sold back to Vickers-Armstrong Ltd on 20 June 1961, being registered G-ARUU. On 5 January 1962, it was sold to the Ministry of Aviation and was rolled out as XR802 in April 1962 in the livery shown here, being delivered to the ETPS at Farnborough on 7 May 1962. Both XR801 and XR802 were withdrawn from use and delivered to Coventry on 18 May 1972, where they were scrapped. Total number of hours flown by XR802 was 18,701. The photograph shows ETPS Viscount, XR802 in its original colour scheme with black cheatline and dayglo trim on finals to Boscombe Down on 13 July 1970. (Photo: Adrian Balch)

(Right:) The first production Westland Scout AH.1, XP165, was used by the ETPS during the '60s and early '70s in this smart red and white scheme, depicted at Boscombe Down on 18 March 1971. (Photo: Adrian Balch)

(Opposite:) A good plan view of the first ETPS SEPECAT Jaguar T.2, XX915, showing the wing markings to advantage. This aircraft was written-off on 17 January 1984, when it crashed into the sea near Poole, Dorset. (Photo: British Aerospace)

(Below:) Currently in use by the Empire Test Pilots' School is Westland Scout AH.1, XP849, which has been at Boscombe Down since delivery on 18 December 1979. It was first seen in the 'raspberry ripple' scheme in 1984 and is still in use by the Rotary Wing Test Squadron. The photograph shows XP849 operating as a crew ferry at Middle Wallop on 6 July 1984. (Photo: Adrian Balch)

THE ROYAL AEROSPACE ESTABLISHMENT

THE EARLY YEARS

The birth of the Establishment can be said to have occurred when the War Office was persuaded by Captain J. L. B. Templer to allocate £150 – the first Air Estimate – for the purpose of building a balloon in the Royal Arsenal at Woolwich. The satisfactory outcome of this venture – a balloon of some 10,000 cubic feet capacity – led to the formation in 1878 of the Balloon Equipment Store, the embryo organisation from which the Royal Flying Corps, Royal Naval Air Service, Royal Air Force, Fleet Air Arm, Army Air Corps as well as the Royal Aircraft and several other Establishments all came. The successful use of observation balloons in various military exercises in the 1880s led to the expansion of the Balloon Equipment Store and its removal, first to the School of Military Engineering at Chatham in 1882 and later, to Aldershot in 1890 to faciliate close co-operation between the Royal Engineers and the British Army. Ascents in India, with campaigns in South Africa and the Sudan, drew attention to the limitations of tethered spherical hydrogen-filled observation balloons.

By 1902, attention was turning toward airship development, and although work was hampered by lack of funds 1905 saw the Balloon Factory on the move to a new and officially temporary site at Farnborough, where space for airship construction and flying was available. Colonel J. E. Capper succeeded Templer as Superintendent and was joined by two of the pioneers of early British aviation, S. F. Cody and Lieutenant J. W. Dunne. The beginning of the Establishment's work on powered aircraft was marked in 1907 by the first flight of British Military Airship No.1 (*Nulli Secondus*).

After some years of experiment with observation and powered kites, Cody, in 1908, constructed a biplane designated as Army Aeroplane No.1 and made the first officially-recorded flight in Britain by a power-driven man-carrying aeroplane on 16 October 1908, being airborne at Farnborough for 496 yards. Cody thus became the first pilot at Farnborough but he and Dunne left in 1909 as the War Office withdrew financial support, having decided that aeroplanes were of no military value. Dunne had, by this time, developed a tailless aircraft that was to be successful.

The Establishment, now carrying the designation of HM Balloon Factory as a consequence of Royal Decree in 1908, entered a new phase with the arrival in 1909 of M. O'Gorman, the first civilian Superintendent, and work concentrated on airship development. The Balloon School RE was separated from the Factory, being renamed as the Air Battalion in 1911 and the Royal Flying Corps in 1912 (with Headquarters at Farnborough until 1915). At the same time HM Balloon Factory, which had been renamed the Army Aircraft Factory in 1911, became the Royal Aircraft Factory

(RAF). In 1910-11 two new aircraft, the SE1 and BE1, were designated and constructed by the Factory. Officially this work was covered by War Office instructions for the repair of a Beriot monoplane, and a Voisin biplane, although in each case the only surviving feature of the original aircraft was the engine. Thus was begun the series of military aeroplanes which was to form the majority of the RFC equipment in 1914-15 and also serve to evolve the basic principles of design, construction, inspection and testing of aircraft which are among the major contributions of RAE to aeronautical engineering. Farnborough began to develop on subject-orientated lines, a theme which has persisted to the present day. F. M. Green and Geoffrey de Havilland joined as Chief Engineer, and designer/test pilot respectively. Up to 1914 the inadequacies of aero engines were a serious handicap and a vigorous research programme began under F. M. Green which resulted eventually in the highly successful RAF series of engines. Captain H. P. T. Lefroy RE, pioneered the use of wireless in airships and aircraft leading to successful transmission of artillery spotting reconnaissance reports by wireless from a BE1 aeroplane in January 1912. The concept of load safety factor and the basic principles of aircraft stressing were established.

WORLD WAR I

The declaration of hostilities in August 1914 finally released the Treasury funds necessary for aeronautical development, but too late for adequate preparation and equipment of the RFC for the early stages of the war. The only British types suitable for production were the Factory's BE, FE and RE designs and the urgent need for their further development resulted in certain functions being transferred to the Testing Squadron of CFS Upavon and the Inspection Dept of the RFC, forerunners of the A&AEE and AQD respectively.

The Factory was expanded rapidly and O'Gorman gathered together a team of brilliant scientists and designers, a list of which reads like a 'Who's Who' of pioneers in British aeronautical science, including names such as F. W. Aston, E. T. Busk, R. H. Mayo, H. P. Folland, H. Glauert, A. A. Griffith, S. Keith Lucas, F. A. Lindermann (later Lord Cherwell), G. I. Taylor and many others. In the period 1914-18 more than 500 aircraft of thirty different types were built, the majority as prototypes for mass production by the newly created and largely inexperienced aircraft industry, which manufactured some 1800 BE2 aircraft in the early war years, and later about 4,000 RE8 artillery reconnaissance aircraft, and finally more than 5,000 SE5A fighters, which were highly successful from 1917 onwards. In 1916 the Government determined that the Factory should concentrate on its present-day functions of research, leaving the manufacturing aspect to industry which was reinforced by the dispersal to it of a number of senior staff from the Factory, many of whom played a prominent part in the subsequent development of British

aviation. At Farnborough rational design procedures and requirements were codified in a six-page pamphlet, issued in 1916, which was the forerunner of the present-day AvP 970 which now extends to three large volumes and defines the requirements for British military fixed-wing aircraft and helicopters. Full scale flight research became closely linked with theoretical work before the war by E. T. Busk's application of the theories developed by G. H. Bryan, leading later to the demonstration of the principles of aircraft spinning and recovery with which the names of Thomson, F. W. Gooden and Lindemann are associated. In 1918 the RFC was retitled as the Royal Air Force and the Factory renamed the Royal Aircraft Establishment to avoid confusion of initials. This change effectively marked the close of an era of which the late Sir Roy Fedden wrote: 'There is no doubt that history has shown that this was a unique place, and you can hardly turn anywhere in British aviation without finding that the good things that were done on aircraft between the two wars stem almost entirely from engineers who had been at this remarkable place and who were inspired by an outstanding leader'.

THE INTER-WAR YEARS

In the inter-war period RAE was handicapped by inadequate availability of resources but despite these difficulties the foundations for later development were laid, particularly in the area of propulsion, where there arose many innovations in piston engine design. In 1926 Griffith formulated the first practical proposal for the use of gas turbines for aircraft propulsion, almost twenty years before their ultimate realisation. Work on pilotless radio-controlled aircraft led steadily towards application to guided weapons, and to the development in 1930 of the Automatic Pilot Mk 1 known as 'George' which became standard equipment on both military and civil aircraft for many years. Co-operation with industry had grown until it became standard practice for aircraft firms to develop their designs with the help of the expertise and facilities at RAE. New facilities were added to keep pace with the increasing performance of aircraft, including a spinning tunnel in 1931 and a 7.2m (24ft) open jet tunnel for near full-scale testing in 1935.

(Right:) Avro 748, XW750, was an early production machine (c/n 1559), which was first delivered to Smith's Aviation Division on 4 December 1963, registered G-ASJT. It was based at Staverton Airport, until the unit closed down on 31 October 1969. G-ASJT was then sold to the Ministry of Technology for operation by the RAE at Farnborough and was delivered on 13 January 1970, becoming XW750. In 1971 it was transferred to RAE Bedford for use by the Blind Landing Experimental Unit and later with the Flight Systems Division. XW750 wore its original Smiths colour scheme with military titles, roundels and serials until 1986 when it was finally given the 'raspberry ripple' treatment. It is seen here flying in September 1987, showing the underside markings to advantage. (Photo: Adrian Balch)

(Below:) Two Auster AOP.9s were operated by the Radio Flight at RAE Farnborough from December 1958 until the mid-70s. WZ672 was built at Rearsby in 1955 and served all its military career in trials work of one form or another. After a brief period stationed at Middle Wallop, it joined RAE Farnborough on 1 December 1958, shortly followed by sister-ship XP277. Both were used by the Radio Flight at Bedford and Farnborough and wore standard Army brown/green camouflage overall with white serials, but devoid of 'Army' titles. In March 1969, the two Austers were given a distinctive overall white scheme with a dark blue cheatline and 'Radio Flight' titles on the nose. After retirement from use with the RAE, WZ672 was acquired by F & H (Aircraft) Ltd, and was registered as G-BDER on 24 June 1975. It was based at Sibson, near Peterborough and retained its RAE colour scheme. It was sold in 1981 and stored until February 1986, when it was sold to the USA. The fate of XP277 is unknown. (RAE Photo).

In 1938-39 design and construction of a pressurised high speed tunnel began; from 1942 this facility played an important part in the development of all British high speed aircraft. A vital contribution was the reconstruction of RAF radio communications, both the ground stations and in the air, where the universally employed medium wave equipment was replaced by a new VHF multi-channel R/T system which proved to be of crucial importance for figher control during the Battle of Britain and in later tactical operations. By the close of the inter-war period once near-insoluble difficulties of control, flutter, aeroelasticity and vibration were beginning to be understood although much more had yet to be done.

WORLD WAR II

At the outbreak of World War II RAE was again expanding rapidly and being rein-forced by many of the country's leading scientists. The scientific and technical output was as versatile as it was effective in contributing to the war effort, many special researches being carried out under extreme urgency and requiring close contact with operational experience. A vital activity was the flight testing of aircraft and equipment both of the Allies and captured machines, including work on detailed performance improvements in crucial areas such as maximum speed and manoeuvrability. Stabilised bomb-sights for high and low altitude bombing and an automatic dead reckoning system for accurate navigation, independent of vulnerable ground aids, were developed and adopted by the RAF and USAAF, as was the highly successful gyro gunsight which resulted in an order of magnitude improvement in the shooting ability of ordinary gunners.

Experiments with a camera-equipped

Spitfire demonstrated the practicability of fast, high altitude reconnaissance aircraft and led to the formation of the RAF Photographic Reconnaissance Unit, subsequently described as the 'indispensable hand-maid of Allied Staffs on every front' – this work also contributed to the widespread post-war use of aerial survey techniques. Other activities included intensive research into the take-off and landing problems of naval aircraft, the techniques and equipment required by the Army Airborne Forces, bomb ballistics, and sea rescue of aircrews; such examples and many others went to the making of RAE's record of war service, much of it achieved in very close collaboration with the appropriate specialised areas of industry.

THE POST-WAR PERIOD

In the immediate post-war lull, all RAE work on piston aero-engines ended and the Engines Department was amalgamated with Power Jets Ltd to form the NGTE as the UK Government centre for research and development in the field of gas turbine engines and their related systems. In 1983 NGTE was recombined as part of RAE. 1945 saw the formation of the Blind Landing Experimental Unit, first at Martlesham Heath and later at Bedford, to begin the development of equipment initially for military aircraft, and culminating with a high integrity automatic landing system for civil transport aircraft, capable of satisfying the stringent requirements of national airworthiness authorities. During 1945-46, a number of exhibitions of wartime aeroplanes were staged at RAE providing the first large-scale public displays of jet aircraft, and in 1948 the SBAC show came to Farnborough for the first time.

Military tension followed rapidly on the heels of a hard won peace, and the atomic

(Below:) The RAE's penultimate Dakota was TS423 (c/n 19347), which served at West Freugh with the Ferranti Flying Unit, with whom it gained this large thimble radar nose. Named 'Mayfly' TS423 was transferred to Farnborough in 1978, then withdrawn from use the following year. It was sold to Aces High Ltd at Duxford and is registered G-DAKS, currently operating out of North Weald, painted as David Lord VC's aircraft, 'KG374'. When with RAE the aircraft wore a white and light grey scheme with blue cheatline, as seen in this photograph, which was taken at Biggin Hill on 22 September 1979. (Photo: Adrian Balch)

warhead, guided weapons rocket and ramjet propulsion heralded an era of high speed flight necessitating the provision of new facilities, particularly for aerodynamics, structures and guided weapons testing. The latter requirements were met initially in 1947 by the establishment of a sea range at Aberporth and a land firing range at Larkhill which became an RAE outstation in 1958. The major development, however, was at Bedford where a complex of powerful new wind tunnels was opened during the period 1951 to 1960, including in 1957 the 2.4m × 2.4m (8ft × 8ft) subsonic and supersonic tunnel with a drive power of 80,000 hp, which has made major contributions to virtually every aerospace project in which there has been UK participation. Other developments at Bedford included provision of a large and fully instrumented airfield having unrestricted approaches, and facilities for catapult and arrester development.

In the most recent twenty-five years of its history RAE has added immeasurably to its achievements across the whole spectrum of aerospace activities but, for reasons of security, and brevity, many topics cannot be described and only a very small sample of the less sensitive developments can be mentioned. The Calvert 'line-and-bar' runway system was originated at RAE, successfully demonstrated on the Berlin Airlift in 1949 and subsequently standardised by ICAO for use throughout the world.

The introduction of PAPI (Precision Approach Path Indicator) and later derivatives typifies a continuing pre-eminence in the field of approach lighting aids. The steam catapult, the angled deck, the hydropneumatic arrester and the mirror landing system are all developments for the safe operation of carrier-borne aircraft to which RAE made major contributions' while vertical take-off research, helicopter development and testing of the ski-jump allowed non-carrier flying from ships to become a reality. In 1954, the Establishment was responsible for the enquiry into the Comet disasters as it had earlier investigated the Tudor accidents and later the Britannia engine icing problems. These established new standards in accident investigation, and new methods for the extensive fatigue testing of pressurised aircraft which were widely adopted in the complex thermal fatigue test on a Concorde airframe at Farnborough, verifying the safe life in advance of airline experience. Perhaps the best known of the recent innovations in materials technology is carbon fibre reinforced plastic which was first developed at RAE in the early 1960s and is finding increasing application on military and civil aircraft and for a variety of diverse non-aerospace applications. During the 1950s, research and development on missiles laid the technological foundation for the successful emergence of a new UK guided-weapon industry. An offshoot of this work included the highly successful Skylark upper atmosphere sounding rocket, developed originally at RAE and subsequently by industry. About 400 successful launches have been made since 1957 in many parts

of the world ranging from the Arctic circle to the Argentine. Later work on ballistic missiles provided the basis for a UK space programme with the development of the Black Arrow rocket and the science research satellite Prospero which was launched in 1971. RAE also played a leading role in the development and operation of a number of research satellites launched from 1967 to 1974 as part of both UK and collaborative programmes, and the British Defence Communications Satellite, Skynet, launched in 1974. Through the 1950s and 1960s flight research with specialised vehicles ranging from the Rolls-Royce 'Flying Bedstead' and Short SC-1, to predecessors of the Harrier, explored the new flight régime of VTOL. The introduction of what was, for their time, novel configurations, such as the Vulcan bomber, Lightning interceptor and Concorde, was aided by exploratory work with research aircraft including the Avro 707, Short SB-5, the BAC 221 and the HP115.

Significant contributions were also made to the development of electrically-signalled controls which were first flown successfully in the mid-1950s, and flight instrumentation was enhanced by the introduction of the head-up-display. Amongst a wealth of achievement in aerodynamics, the most significant single development in recent years was the conception in the mid-1950s of the slender wing aircraft with controlled flow separations, leading directly to the design adopted for Concorde. This mighty achievement involved half a working lifetime for many, particularly that of the late Dietrich Kuchemann.

Multi-national ventures such as the Jaguar and Tornado weapons systems and Concorde, provide an illustration of the contrasting nature of various aspects of the research and development programme which supported them. RAE contributions to these projects have ranged from elegant intellectual hypotheses to design refinement via thousands of hours of development in massive test facilities, to equally vital, if more down to earth, research on basic topics such as the properties of materials, adhesives and fasteners, the accuracy and integrity of avionic systems, and a host of other factors which affect the safety of the airframe and the provision of a suitable environment for the occupants of a vehicle capable of travelling at around 1400 mph in the stratosphere. From this account it is possible to discern, if only sketchily, the essential part which the former Royal Aircraft Establishment continues to play in aerospace research. RAE provides the knowledge for the armoury of missiles and aircraft necessary to national defence, and helps to sustain a UK capability for advanced civil aircraft which is vital for our future prosperity.

In May 1989, the Royal Aircraft Establishment was renamed the Royal Aerospace Establishment, to reflect its avionics and space work. However, only a few of the aircraft have adopted the new titles, even after four years.

Since 1991, RAE has been part of the new

Defence Research Agency and as such continues to direct the greater part of its effort into meeting the future requirements of the Armed Forces, but increasingly the broadening of aeronautical research will encourage more support for civil aviation and space projects.

(Left:) BAC One-Eleven Srs. 201AC, XX105, was only the fourth production One-Eleven built (c/n 8) and began life as G-ASJD, making its first flight on 6 July 1964 from Bournemouth-Hurn Airport. However, a little over a month later it was involved in an accident during flight testing. The BAC test pilot, Peter Baker, recovering the aircraft from an intentional 'deep stall', which had proved fatal to an earlier aircraft and crew, was able to carry out a remarkable forced landing on Salisbury Plain.

The aircraft suffered little damage and, after removal by road to BAC Hurn, it was rejigged in the workshops to fly again ten months later in June 1965. Resplendent with black cheat line and red lettering, it was delivered to British United Airways at Gatwick on 5 August 1965. For the next six years, G-ASJD flew thousands of holiday-makers around Europe. In 1967, BUA changed their livery to incorporate a blue and tan-brown cheat line. A further colour scheme change came in December 1970, when British United merged with Caledonian Airways to form British Caledonian Airlines. The aircraft was sold to MoD(PE) on 21 September 1971 and returned to BAC Hurn on 1 October 1971 for overhaul and to be refurbished for the Blind Landing Experimental Unit (BLEU). It was obtained as a replacement for the RAE's Comet 2E, XN453, and their Comet 3B, XP915.

Registered XX105, it was flown to Cranfield Institute of Technology in February 1972, where changes were made to the autopilot installation to suit BLEU research requirements. UHF radio equipment was also fitted, together with a new flight system – Collins (FD 108) – similar to that of the 500 Series One-Eleven. BAC installed an Analogue computer to provide a 'versatile autopilot' facility. Also Direct Lift Control (DLC) has been fitted by BAC Hurn.

Initially, flying was shared – Aerodynamics Flight Department studying the manual use of DLC in the approach and landing phase, while BLEU considered the benefits to be gained from advanced automatic control laws in the same area with and without DLC compared with the present generation of autopilots. The feasibility of making automatic landings from steeper than normal approaches as a means of noise reduction has also been studied. This work has lead to an assessment of some of the implications of STOL operations, proposed new guidance systems and automation in the terminal movements area.

The aircraft is in a striking red, yellow and white livery and wore 'Blind Landing Experimental Unit' roof titles (top) until the end of 1977, when this was changed to 'Royal Aircraft Establishment' (bottom). XX105 is currently devoid of titles and spends its time between Farnborough and Bedford on trials. (RAE Photos)

THE ROYAL SIGNALS & RADAR ESTABLISHMENT

(Below:) BAC One-Eleven Srs. 402AaP, XX919 (c/n 21), first flew from Bournemouth-Hurn as PI-C1121 on 7 April 1966 and was delivered to Philippine Air Lines on 19 April 1966. It was sold back to BAC in December 1971, who sold it to MoD(PE) for use by RAE Farnborough. It was delivered as XX919 on 16 May 1974, being painted with a dark blue cheatline on a white and grey fuselage. It is seen here in this scheme on finals to Brize Norton on 11 July 1978. (Photo: Adrian Balch).

The former RSRE site at Malvern near Worcester, now part of the Defence Research Agency, is the main centre for MOD work on electronic systems and devices. Research is carried out on new electronic devices and their innovative application, which provides the key to radical developments in electronic equipment for all the Services. Supported by the Department of Industry, the main systems activities in RSRE are airborne, battlefield and ground radar, opto-electronics, guided weapons, ground-based communications and air traffic control, the latter being funded by the Civil Aviation Authority. In all aspects, the Establishment conducts the research through to the initiation and assessment of new system concepts and thence to supporting the Procurement Executive, Ministry of Defence during the development by industry of electronic equipment for the Services.

The origins of RSRE may be traced back to 1903, when the Army chose two men to develop the military potential of wireless telegraphy and posted them to the School of Military Engineering at Chatham. Develop-

ment of this work was so dramatic, in the next eight years that an Experimental Wireless Telegraphy Section of the Royal Engineers was formed. In 1914, it moved to Woolwich Dockyard and during World War I re-established itself on Woolwich Common as the Signals Experimental Establishment.

Although concentrating on the development of wireless telegraphy the Establishment, even in those early days, experimented with methods of direction and range-finding. But by the end of the war the staff was reduced and the effort was confined to the adaption of signals techniques to the needs of a mechanised Army.

The rearmament programme of 1935-9, however, brought new responsibilities and, with a rapidly increasing staff during World War II, it was decided to transfer to Christchurch, where work continued under the title of the Signals Research and Development Establishment (SRDE).

During the war important advances were made in mine detection techniques and in radio equipment for tropical and jungle warfare. One of the establishment's major achievements was the development of the multi-channel microwave link, known as the 'No.10 Set', which played an important part in the invasion of Europe in 1944 and in other theatres of war.

(Below:) XX919 remained in this colour scheme until 1983, when it appeared in the red, white and blue 'raspberry ripple' scheme at the International Air Tattoo at Greenham Common in July of that year. It currently flies in this scheme from Farnborough and Bedford. XX919 is seen in its current colour scheme during a visit to its birth place – Bournemouth-Hurn, on 3 June 1988. At the time of writing, it had yet to have its roof titles amended from 'Aircraft' to 'Aerospace'. (Photo: Adrian Balch)

At about the beginning of the pre-war rearmament programme Robert Watson Watt, who was later knighted for his scientific work, suggested that the radio techniques which he was investigating at the Department of Scientific and Industrial Research might be capable of detecting aircraft in flight. This suggestion proved to be the birth of radar, which played a vital part in the Battle of Britain and other air operations of World War II. Watt verified his theories to the satisfaction of the Air Ministry by demonstrating that electromagnetic energy broadcast from the ground could be reflected by an aircraft and received back at the point of transmission.

With this evidence, the Air Ministry founded a research establishment, first at Orfordness and later at Bawdsey Manor, Suffolk. Initially, its task was to develop and install a chain of early warning radar stations around the coastline of Britain. The first of these was handed over to the Royal Air Force in May 1937, and by the beginning of World War II twenty stations had been completed.

At the outbreak of war, the Air Ministry side was transferred, first to Dundee and then to Swanage, where it continued as the newly-formed Telecommunications Research Establishment (TRE). The War Office team moved to Christchurch to join an Air Defence Research and Development Establishment, which later became the Radar Research and Development Establishment (RRDE).

TRE continued its pioneering work of developing radars for the ground controlled interception of enemy aircraft and for airborne attack in fighter aircraft. Airborne radars were also developed for attacking submarines and ships and as navigation and target mapping aids for the bombing offensive in Europe. Meanwhile, RRDE concentrated on developing radars for anti-aircraft and coastal defence guns. Mobile equipment was also developed for the detection of approaching aircraft and the location of enemy mortars by the Army.

In 1942, the first steps were taken to concentrate electronic research and development for the Services at Malvern. In that year, TRE and RRDE moved to Worcestershire. The two establishments at Malvern retained their separate identities until 1953, when they were amalgamated to form the Radar Research Establishment. During a visit by Her Majesty the Queen to Malvern in 1957 the title was changed to the Royal Radar Establishment.

Associated flying trials were conducted from nearby Pershore airfield, until 1976 when the three Establishments were amalgamated as the Royal Signals and Radar Establishment. Work at Malvern continues to this day in new buildings which were formally opened by His Royal Highness Prince Edward, Duke of Kent, on 4 December 1980. However, Pershore airfield was closed and the fleet of aircraft was moved to Bedford and took up residence there in April 1977 under the wing of RAE.

RSRE and RAE now both form part of the Defence Research Agency.

(Right:) XB259 was the first production Blackburn Beverley and the last to be retired. It first flew from Brough on 29 January 1955 and was used by Blackburns for early ROTAG trials. It was allocated registration G-AOAI, but this was never carried and the aircraft was later delivered to the RAE at Farnborough on 16 September 1959 for parachute drop-load development trials, although it was used by the ETPS as No. '17' for a short time. During the early 1960s, XB259 had its wings and fuselage undersides painted yellow with black stripes, in the manner of target-towing aircraft. Moveable surfaces were natural metal, as were the fuselage sides and top of the wings. Underneath the boom was painted black, and a black and white stripe was painted along the fuselage for photographic trials. The cabin top was white with the usual anti-dazzle patch of black. The leading edges of the wings were light grey. Dayglo red was used on the nose, wingtips, tailplanes, and spinners. Unfortunately, no colour photographs have been located showing this interesting scheme.

In 1966, XB259 was repainted gloss white overall with black engines and orange dayglo nose, spinners, underside of the wingtips and outer surfaces of the vertical fins. By 1971 the orange dayglo areas had become faded, so were over-painted in matt orange paint. At this time, the engine cowlings were natural metal and the spinners black, the tip of the nose also being black.

XB259 served all its life at RAE Farnborough and was retired at the end of 1972. It was bought by the long-defunct holiday airline, Court-Line, who were going to use it to ferry engines and large spares around Europe from Luton. However, this airline was in financial trouble and the deal fell through. XB259 made its last flight on 30 March 1977, when it flew to Hull-Paull for preservation and use as a club house. It later moved on to the Army Museum of Transport at Beverley, Yorkshire, where it resides today, the sole Beverley extant.

XB259 is seen here during a visit to Hatfield on 7 October 1971. (Photo: Dick Winfield)

(Below:) XN923 was the second production Buccaneer S.Mk.1, which also spent its entire life on trials work. It immediately went to the A&AEE at Boscombe Down in 1963 until 1965 and retained its original overall white anti-radiation scheme. In 1967, it was passed on to the RAE at Farnborough, where it gained a dark blue fin and band round the nose. The nose-cone was dayglo red, as were the wingtips and two bands across the fin, alongside which was the RAE crest. XN923 spent most of its life at Farnborough, where it was fitted with detachable noses for equipment development. It continued flying from Farnborough until 1973, when it was retired to Boscombe Down for ground use. It was bought by a private collector in 1990 and was transferred to a site near Gatwick Airport, where it resides today, its future uncertain. XN923 is seen here at Coltishall on 19 September 1970, during the station's Battle of Britain Open Day. (Photo: Bob Griggs)

(Right:) XN975 was the second production S.Mk.2 Buccaneer and has been one of the most elusive to date. Seen here retaining its original Fleet Air Arm dark grey and white scheme with orange (not dayglo) extremities, it served with the Royal Radar Establishment at Pershore, Worcs. It is seen there in 1976, involved in radar trials, but its future and current status are unknown. (Photo: via Peter Middlebrook)

(Below:) Buccaneer S.2A, XT272, has spent all its life on research and development work. In 1977 it was modified with a Tornado GR.1 nose by British Aerospace at Brough and currently spends its time between British Aerospace at Warton and RAE Bedford. Initially painted extra dark sea grey overall with orange dayglo trim, this aircraft has since been repainted in the 'raspberry ripple' scheme. It is seen here taxying out at Warton in October 1977.

Note that the rear portion of the canopy is blacked out for radar trials. (Photo: Patrick Little)

(Right:) Before being transferred to A&AEE, Canberra B(I)6, WT309 served with the RAE at Bedford in this white and red (not dayglo) scheme (compare with photos on pages 18/19). It is seen here in August 1979, just after being transferred from one Establishment to the other. (Photo: Adrian Balch)

(Top left:) Operated by the Blind Landing Experimental Unit, this was the RAE's most elusive Comet 2E, XV144. It was originally delivered to BOAC as G-AMXK in August 1957, but was soon transferred to the Ministry of Supply on 12 October 1960. It was delivered to RAE Bedford on 18 November 1966 then was transferred to Farnborough on 18 May 1971. In 1974, it was withdrawn from use and finally broken up at Farnborough in August 1975. (Photo: RAE Bedford)

(Centre left:) This photograph of the Canberra PR.9 prototype, WH793, was taken at Luqa, Malta, on 11 November 1968, when the aircraft was painted with a different pattern of dayglo red to that shown in the later photograph on the right. (Photo: Dave Lawrence)

Delivered to the Ministry of Supply on 26 May 1954, WH793 began life as a Canberra PR.7, but was later converted to the PR.9 prototype on 8 July 1955 and delivered to the RAE. After conversion for evaluation of the wing planform of the later PR.9, WH793 was given a liberal application of dayglo red patches and joined the Bedford Aero Flight, who fitted it with a gust response boom. It was used by the Meteorological Research Flight and flew worldwide on gust and thunderstorm research, during which it acquired the nose-art on its starboard side. It was also used as a Concorde chase plane and it is seen here in that role at Fairford on 1 August 1974, with close-up of the nose-art (bottom left). WH793 was scrapped in August 1975. (Photos: Adrian Balch)

(Below:) One of the best examples of co-operation between the relevant manufacturer and the RRE was hybrid Canberra B.2/8, WJ643 which was used by Ferranti supported by teams from the RRE. This aircraft joined the flying unit at Turnhouse in 1954, as a B.2. Its first task was to act as an airborne target for the Airpass radar installed in the nose of Dakota TS423. Within two years the Canberra was at Seighford where Boulton Paul replaced its original nose with that of a B.8. This too having been converted, carrying as it did a complete Airpass unit in the nose. In its new guise, WJ643 first flew in January 1958 when it returned to Turnhouse. WJ643 carried out Airpass testing until 1964, after which it was modified to carry a Ferranti-designed INAS system. As this programme required a lot of low flying, WJ643 was fitted with a pair of B(I)8 wings, complemented by a pair of increased thrust Avon 109 engines. Now close to B(I)8 standard, WJ643 resumed flying in 1966. The INAS development and trials programme continued in support of the Harrier until December 1969, after which the aircraft was flown to Farnborough for further modification. The following year, WJ643 emerged ready for a new development programme, combining RAE/RRE/Ferranti effort entailing the fitting of a Laser Ranger and Marked Target Seeker (LRMTS) that was being developed for the forthcoming Jaguar. Once modified, this Canberra was resprayed silver and covered in liberal amounts of dayglo. In this guise, WJ643 flew from the weapons test range at West Freugh. LRMTS trials continued for the Tornado until 22 September 1972, when it returned to the RAE at Farnborough. It was then painted in the RAE's white, grey and blue scheme shown in the photograph and was employed on electro-optic sensor research and other duties. About 1978 it was painted in the 'raspberry ripple' colour scheme, in which it performed limited duties until it was withdrawn from use and dismantled at Farnborough in November 1981. The photograph shows WJ643 over its home base of RAE Farnborough on 11 January 1975. (RAE photo)

(Right:) Wing colour scheme details are shown to effect in this view of RAE Canberra B.2, WK163 from Bedford, alongside A&AEE Canberra B(I)6, WT309. In the distance is RAE Farnborough's Comet 4, XV814 all of which formed part of the static display at the TVS Air Show South at Bournemouth-Hurn on 17 August 1984. (Photo: Adrian Balch)

(Below:) WH734 was transferred from RAF charge to Flight Refuelling Ltd on 31 July 1954 and was used for in-flight refuellng in conjunction with A&AEE for the next twenty-odd years, spending its time between Tarrant Rushton and Boscombe in a plain overall silver scheme. Since then, Flight Refuelling have modified it to TT.18 target-tug standard, following which the undersides were painted in the traditional black and yellow diagonal stripes. As part of the Mod(PE) fleet, WH734 operates from RAE Llanbedr and has adopted the 'raspberry ripple' scheme, but retains the black/yellow target-tug stripes underneath, making it the most colourful Canberra in current service. It is seen here at Leuchars on 17 September 1988. (Photo: W.F. Wilson)

(Bottom:) One of many Canberras operated by the Royal Radar Establishment from Pershore, Worcs. was PR.7, WH774. It has spent all its life on radar research trials since being taken on charge on 31 August 1955. Wearing an overall silver finish with dayglo trim, WH774 wore the RRE badge on its fin until being transferred to Bedford in 1977, on the closure of Pershore. In 1982 it was repainted in the 'raspberry ripple' scheme at Kemble and was involved in missile linescan trials at Bedford. WH774 was withdrawn from use at Farnborough in 1988, then scrapped there. The photograph shows it arriving at Abingdon on 15 September 1972 for the annual Battle of Britain air display. Even in its original silver colour scheme, it was in pristine condition. Note the radar 'bump' above the forward fuselage. (Photos: Adrian Balch)

(Left:) Possibly the most famous test-bed Canberra of all time must be the specially converted Shorts SC.9, which had been on the production line at Belfast as a normal PR.9 until its role was changed. Acquired mainly for missile seeker head testing, XH132 was used by the missile divisions of de Havilland and Hawker Siddeley Dynamics before progressing through the RRE to its last owners the RAE. During its career, the aircraft has been modified with a tripled-pronged nose and modified pods on the wingtips. Used for development of the Red Top and other missiles, XH132 was painted white overall with black extreme rear fuselage and nose. By 1974, it had been passed on to the RRE at Pershore for radar development trials. It was repainted silver overall with small amounts of dayglo trim. When Pershore closed in 1977, XH132 was transferred to Bedford and by 1982 had been repainted in the 'raspberry ripple' scheme. It was retired to the BDRF at St Mawgan on 24 September 1986, where it was given a hemp and grey colour scheme prior to being scrapped in 1992. The photograph shows a close-up of the modified nose of Canberra SC.9, XH132, when painted white overall with Hawker Siddeley Dynamics at Hatfield on 5 July 1969. (Photo: Adrian Balch).

(Below:) This photograph shows Canberra SC.9, XH132, in the 'raspberry ripple' scheme when with RAE Bedford, seen on finals to Greenham Common on 21 July 1983 for the International Air Tattoo. (Photo: Adrian Balch)

(Below:) De Havilland Comet 2E, XN453 was built as G-AMXD, the fourth Comet 2 for BOAC being rolled out in 1954. The designation 2E resulted from the aircraft being re-engined with Avon 504s in the inner positions and the larger Avon 524s in the outer nacelles. After route-proving trials for the introduction of the Comet 4 in 1957, it was taken over by RAE Farnborough, its interior completely reworked as a radio workshop. Radio equipment was carried in a pod under the nose and XN453 was flown extensively all over the world in the development of long-range radio-navigation aids until being withdrawn from use in February 1973 and broken up at Farnborough. Initially white and silver with a black cheatline, the last three years of its life saw all silver areas repainted light grey. The photograph shows XN453 visiting Linton-on-Ouse on 19 July 1971. (Photo: Dave Lawrence)

(Right:) As part of the abortive Nimrod AEW.3 programme, ex-BOAC Comet 4, G-APDS, was acquired for the development of the Marconi radar on 30 January 1969, initially based at Boscombe Down. It was delivered to Woodford for the addition of the nose radome and officially rolled out on 1 March 1977. On completion of its part of the development programme, XW626 was delivered to RAE Bedford. To balance the modified nose, a Nimrod's fin was added. The colour scheme was similar to that on XS235, with the addition of titles on the roof and lower forward fuselage. When the Nimrod AEW.3 was cancelled, XW626 was made redundant and was retired from use at Bedford, making its last flight on 28 August 1981. At the time of writing, it is still there, providing a nesting place for several birds on the airfield. The photograph shows XW626 at the Farnborough Air Show on 6 September 1978. (Photo: Adrian Balch)

(Below:) BAC 221, WG774, was converted from one of the two world speed record breaking Fairey Delta 2s at Filton in 1964. Prior to conversion, WG774 broke the World Speed Record on 10 March 1956 with a speed of 1,132 mph. It was converted with a Concorde-shaped wing for high-speed research trials. It was employed by the Aerodynamics Flight at RAE Bedford until 1974, following which it was delivered to the Scottish Museum of Flight at East Fortune. It was later passed on to the Fleet Air Arm Museum at Yeovilton, where it currently resides alongside Concorde 002. (BAe)

(Below:) The unique Handley Page HP.115, XP841, was built to a Ministry of Aviation contract for research into low-speed handling characteristics of slender delta-wing aircraft. Powered by a single Bristol Siddeley Viper 9 turbojet engine, XP841 first flew on 17 August 1961 and provided much valuable data for the development of Concorde. It had a fixed under-carriage and the fairing at the top of the fin contained a camera to photograph wool tufts on the wing during flight testing. It was flown intensively by pilots of the RAE at Bedford, to study stability, control and handling character-istics. It remained at Bedford for all its life, being retired in late 1973 and flown to Colerne on 1 February 1974 for the museum there. It was taken by road to Cosford on 9 October 1975, then transferred to its present resting place, the Concorde Museum at Yeovilton in 1979. The HP.115 was natural metal overall apart from black/white photographic discs on the nose and fin. 'RAE Bedford AERO FLIGHT' appeared in small red letters on the nose. The photograph shows XP841 near Bedford in 1969. (Photo: RAE Bedford)

(Right:) The RAE Air Transport Flight's De Havilland Devon quartet from left to right, VP975/M, XG496/K, VP959/L and XM223/J. Photographed near Farnborough in 1976, these four Devons served with the RAE from the early '50s until retirement in February 1986, when they were replaced by Piper PA-31 Navajo-Chieftains. (Photo: RAE Bedford)

(Bottom:) De Havilland Devon C.2, VP959/L, was one of a quartet operated by RAE Farnborough's Air Transport Flight for all its life, being delivered on 30 June 1958 until 1965, when it went to Llanbedr. It returned to Farnborough in January 1971 coded 'L' and was converted to a Mk.2. When Farnborough's Devon fleet was replaced by Piper Navajo-Chieftains in 1985, VP959 was transferred to RAE West Freugh. The photograph shows Devon C.2, VP959 in its original blue, white and yellow colour scheme visiting its birthplace of Hatfield on 13 November 1973. (Photo: Dick Winfield)

(Below:) De Havilland Devon C.2, WB530, was operated by RAE Bedford for a period in the '60s after serving with the Idris Station Flight. During its period with RAE, it adopted a liberal amount of dayglo as shown in this photograph taken at Woodford in April 1968. It went on to serve with 21 and 207 squadrons and was retired to Swinderby in 1984, where it was preserved for a while but finally burned by the Fire Section there in 1988. (Photo: Iain MacPherson)

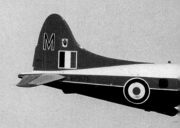

(Below:) RAE Farnborough's Douglas Dakota C3, ZA947, was initially painted as 'KG661' when delivered to West Freugh in May 1971, MoD(PE) mistakenly identifying ex CAF 661 as the one-time RAF Dakota KG661. However, in 1979, it was pointed out to them that the real KG661 crashed in December 1944 and that Canadian Air Force 661 was c/n 10200 and not ill-fated c/n 13478. Named 'Portpatrick Princess', 'KG661' was repainted as ZA947 in July 1979, with a later serial than some Tornados. With both serials, it wore the white and grey scheme with blue cheatline, as shown in the photograph as 'KG661' at Abingdon on 15 September 1978. (Photo: Adrian Balch)

(Right:) Dakota C3, ZA947, was repainted in the 'raspberry ripple' scheme in 1984 and was used for trials of low speed sensing equipment, RPVs and parachutes, as well as for general transport duties. On 8 August 1989 the wing was badly damaged when the port undercarriage collapsed, but a replacement wing was obtained and ZA947 served as the last Dakota in British military markings until being withdrawn from use in early 1993 and transferred to the RAF's Battle of Britain Memorial Flight as a support aircraft. It is seen here landing at Abingdon in September 1985. (Photo: Adrian Balch)

(Below:) The only Nimrod to adopt a non-standard colour scheme was MR.1, XV148, which was the first of its type to fly and retained an almost full complement of Comet windows. When with RAE Bedford, XV148 was given a red (not dayglo) rear fuselage and wingtips as seen in this photograph taken visiting Kinloss on 19 February 1982. It is now withdrawn from use and in use with Woodford's Fire Section. (Photo: Robbie Shaw)

(Right:) Dakota C3, ZA947, is seen here over its home base of Farnborough in formation with the three RAE Navajo-Chieftains during 1986. (Photo: RAE)

(Below:) Handley Page Hastings C.2, WD480, was operated by RAE Farnborough during the 1960s, gaining a large under-fuselage pannier for avionics and radar trials. By the early '70s, the RAE had standardised the colour scheme to white and light grey with blue trim as seen here on WD480 during a visit to Lyneham on 27 April 1973. This aircraft was struck off charge and scrapped at Farnborough the following year. (Photo: Brian Shields)

(Right:) This standard Dominie T.1, XS738, leads this RAE formation while on loan to Farnborough. Nearest the camera is Hastings C.2, WD480, modified with under-fuselage pannier, with Comet 4 XX944. This Comet was originally delivered to BOAC as G-APDP and was purchased from Dan-Air in July 1973. It was used for less than two years by RAE, being withdrawn from use in April 1975, so photographs of it in RAE markings are seldom seen. This photograph was taken from the RAE's ill-fated Meteor T.7, XF274, on a sortie out of Farnborough on 1 October 1973. (Photo: Jeremy Flack).

(Left:) HS-125 Srs.1B, XW930, was built at Chester in 1965 for the John Bloom empire of Rolls-Razor with c/n 25009. After a lengthy period in storage, it was registered G-ATPC to the Ministry of Aviation on 11 February 1966, for use by the Civil Aviation Flying Unit (CAFU) at Stansted. On 7 December 1970, it was transferred to the RAE at Bedford to become XW930. It has been involved in the study of environmental phenomena such as low-level turbulence, wind-shear, vortex-wakes and thunderstorm activity. Fitted with an instrumentation nose probe for recording data, XW930 was painted in a white and metallic green scheme with red cheatline. It was then used for engine noise suppression trials and led to development of the 'hush-kit'. By 1983, XW930 had been repainted white and grey with blue cheatline and red fin. Ferranti fitted a laser nose to the aircraft for Laser True Airspeed Systems (LATAS) trials. During the next modification for Blue Vixen radar trials, XW930 was repainted in the 'raspberry ripple' scheme, emerging with Sea Harrier FRS.2's nose painted red, giving XW930 the nickname 'Rudolph'. Trials began on 14 September 1988 and the aircraft is in this configuration today, although the red nose cone has been replaced by one painted light grey. The photograph shows HS-125, XW930 in its first RAE colour scheme with 'toasting fork' instrumentation probe, on finals to Bedford on 22 March 1973. (Photo: Adrian Balch)

(Below:) HS-125, XW930, in its current guise with Sea Harrier FRS.2 nose for Blue Vixen radar trials, seen at Fairford in July 1987. (Photo: Adrian Balch)

(Opposite): The Royal Radar Establishment at Pershore used hybrid Meteor NF.11, WD790, for a variety of trials and was fitted with a TSR.2's nose cone for trials involving the radar intended for that type. When Pershore closed, WD790 transferred to RAE Bedford in April 1977, becoming the only Meteor to adopt the 'raspberry ripple' colour scheme in which it is seen here flying from Bedford on 3 November 1981. Regretfully, WD790 was scrapped at Leeming in February 1982 in order to keep the 'Vintage Pair' Meteor flying. However, the nose survived and went to the North East Air Museum at Sunderland, Tyne & Wear. (Photo: RAE Bedford)

(Below:) The Radar Research Establishment at Pershore used the hybrid Meteor NF.11, WD790, for a variety of trials, including testing the radar intended for the TSR.2, hence the odd nose radome. It was modified to NF.12 standard, so was unofficially called an NF.11½. When Pershore closed in 1977. WD790 was transferred to RAE Llanbedr, then to Bedford. It was operated in grey and green camouflage with silver undersides when seen here at St Mawgan for the Battle of Britain Open Day on 18 September 1971. (Photo: Stephen Wolf)

(Right:) Two Meteor T.7s were operated by the RAE in this smart, blue, white and grey colour scheme. Employing them as chase-planes and hacks, Farnborough operated the ill-fated XF274 which crashed in 1975 and Llanbedr operated WA662, which was delivered from the Fighter Command Comms Squadron at Bovingdon on 17 March 1958. Initially operated in an overall silver scheme with yellow trainer bands and coded 'K', WA662 was repainted in 1978 and continued to serve as a 'shepherd' aircraft for the pilotless drones operating out of Llanbedr. In 1989 it was withdrawn from use and delivered to Chalgrove for use as a spares ship by Martin-Baker Ltd. In 1993 it was moved to a private collector near Derby. The photograph shows WA662 on finals to Greenham Common on 22 July 1983 for the last International Air Tattoo to be held at that venue. (Photo: Adrian Balch)

(Below:) Gloster Meteor D.16, WH453/L, was one of the last two Meteor drones used by the Defence Research Agency at Llanbedr, at the time of writing. In its smart conspicuous red and yellow colour scheme, it is seen taxying out at Fairford on 24 July 1989, after participating in the static park of the International Air Tattoo. (Photo: Adrian Balch)

A shaft of sunlight illuminates RAE Vickers Varsity R.1, WF379, against a stormy sky at Abingdon on 15 September 1978. With its elongated radar nose, this aircraft served on radar trials with RRE Pershore from October 1954 and later at RAE Bedford before it was scrapped. Apart from the additon of roof titles, its colour scheme remained unchanged. (Photo: Adrian Balch)

ZF521 is one of a trio of Piper PA-31 Navajo-Chieftains currently operated by RAE Farnborough's Air Transport Flight, which replaced four Devons in 1985. ZF521 was built in 1978 and used by a hydro company near Oklahoma, registered N27509. It came to RAE with a flying time of 1,350 hours and currently flies alongside ZF520 and ZF522. The photograph shows ZF521 viewed under the tail of ZF522 while waiting for pilots delivering aircraft to the static park of Air Tournament 92 at Boscombe Down on 12 June 1992. (Photo: Adrian Balch)

(Below:) Short SC.1, XG900, was one of a pair built for vertical take-off and landing (VTOL) jet research. Powered by five 200lb thrust, Rolls-Royce RB.108 engines – four for vertical lift and one for conventional flight – XG900 first flew on 4 February 1957. It joined RAE Bedford in April 1961 and retained its overall natural metal finish with orange dayglo rudder and wingtips. It continued to fly from Bedford for the next ten years, finally being retired and presented to the Science Museum on 22 June 1971. After a brief spell on display at South Kensington, XG900 was put in store at Hayes until it was transferred to Wroughton in 1987, followed by a further transfer to the Fleet Air Arm Museum at Yeovilton in 1989, where it is currently displayed alongside other British vertical take-off jet pioneering aircraft. The photograph shows SC.1, XG900, outside the Science Museum's store in Hayes on 6 June 1989. (Photo: Adrian Balch)

(Right:) XG905 was the other Short SC.1, which was the first to fly vertically, while XG900 was the first to fly conventionally. XG905 made its first public appearance at the Farnborough Air Show in September 1959. The first transition from vertical to horizontal flight was made on 6 April 1960 from RAE Bedford. XG905 was used for all-weather and night-flying trials by the Blind Landing Experimental Unit and was also withdrawn from use in 1971. It was donated to the Ulster Folk and Transport Museum at Belfast in May 1974, where it resides today. The photograph of XG905 shows the underside markings to advantage. (Photo: RAE)

(Below:) Westland Sea King Mk.4X, ZB506, was delivered to RAE Bedford in 1982, followed by ZB507 to RAE Farnborough. Used for radar trials, these helicopters are modified HC.4s with a fixed undercarriage, coupled with Sea King HAS.5 radomes. Since 1986, ZB506 has been involved in trials with the Blue Kestrel radar being developed for the EH.101 Merlin helicopter. This gives it the distinctive 'platypus-shaped' nose. The photograph shows ZB506 at Fairford on 22 July 1989 during the International Air Tattoo.

(Right:) Close-up of the Blue Kestrel radar nose on Sea King Mk.4X, ZB506, being developed by Ferranti for the EH.101 Merlin. (Photos: Adrian Balch)

(Left:) The unique Hawker Hunter T.12, XE531, began life as an F.Mk.6, then was converted to an FGA.9 and finally to a two-seater with head-up display and vertical camera nose, givng it the designation T.Mk.12. In 1973, XE531 began trials with a fly-by-wire system and on 19 February 1980, it arrived at Holme-on-Spalding-Moor for use in a joint RAE/BAe flight test programme to study fly-by-wire controls. Unfortunately, this smart green and white Hunter Mk.12 crashed on take-off from Farnborough on 17 March 1982. The photograph shows XE531 at Greenham Common on 1 July 1976 during the International Air Tattoo's Hunter 25th Anniversary celebrations. (Photo: John Hughes)

(Bottom:) Hawker Hunter T.7, XF321, served with Nos 56 and 8/43 Squadrons before joining the RAE at Farnborough, painted in the 'raspberry ripple' scheme. It flew until 1985, when it was withdrawn from use and transferred to RNEC Manadon for ground instructional use. The photograph shows XF321 visiting Odiham on 27 July 1987, with RAE Bedford's BAC One-Eleven, XX919 behind. (Photo: Stephen Wolf)

(Below:) Hawker Hunter F.6, XG210, was operated by RAE Bedford on missile development work and was fitted with an FR.10 camera nose to film the trials. Initially flown in standard camouflage, it appeared in the 'raspberry ripple' scheme by 1981. Frequently flown from Hatfield, in association with Hawker Siddeley Dynamics, XG210 also spent much time at Dunsfold and was finally retired in 1986 to the RAE Apprentice School at Bedford. The photograph shows XG210 at Hatfield on 6 July 1985. (Photo: Adrian Balch)

(Below:) Avro Shackleton MR.3, WR972, was initially used by Avros at Woodford for various development trials work. It was fitted with a ventral rescue lifeboat under the fuselage bomb-bay and was in this configuration when the trials were continued at the A&AEE Boscombe Down in 1959/60. It was delivered to the SME Flt at Farnborough on 13 April 1961 for parachute drag trials and was fitted with a special rear fuselage blunt turret and parachute deploy mechanism. Although originally in the standard RAF Coastal Command grey colour scheme, after arrival at Farnborough it was painted silver overall with dayglo orange nose, wingtips and fins. The undersides of the wings were painted yellow with black diagonal stripes as was the underside of the fuselage, in target-tug manner. In March 1968 the colour scheme was revised to conform with a standard RAE-type scheme – white upper surfaces (including wings), light grey lower surfaces, with a blue cheatline and fins, and various black and white areas. Towards the end of its life, WR972 was engaged in miscellaneous parachute trials and was finally broken up at Farnborough in 1973. The photograph shows Shackleton MR.3, WR972, at Coltishall on 14 September 1968. (Photo: Author's collection)

(Right:) Avro Shackleton T.4, VP293, was built as an MR.1 in 1950 at Woodford, Manchester and served with several squadrons until 1956, when it was converted to a T.4. After service with the Maritime Operational Training Unit at Kinloss it joined the RAE at Farnborough in 1964 for use by the Weapons Flight. It retained the standard RAF Coastal Command dark sea grey scheme with white roof until the early 1970s, when the extremities were painted orange dayglo, which was later overpainted in plain matt orange paint, as the dayglo started fading and was looking very patchy. The propellor blades were painted in black/white anti-collision stripes as a safety measure. Around the early 1970s, No.8 Squadron's Shackleton AEW.2s began appearing with names of characters from the BBC TV children's series, 'The Magic Roundabout'. VP293 became named 'Zebedee' for several reasons – many of the little black boxes that it carried had to be harnessed inside the Shackleton's notoriously noisy and shaky fuselage on springs. The aircraft was also prone to being bounced on landing, so it was inevitable that VP293 would become 'Zebedee' and this character was proudly portrayed on the aircraft's sides and on the extreme rear. Retired from service in 1975, 'Zebedee' flew into Strathallan on 3 May 1976 for preservation. Constant exposure to the Scottish weather took its toll on the airframe and VP293 had to be broken up in 1988. (Photo: RAE)

(Bottom right:) The photograph shows Shackleton T.4, VP293, when on display at Strathallan on 11 September 1977. (Photo: Richard Hamblin)

(Below:) One of several Westland Wessex helicopters used by RAE Farnborough was this HAS.1, XM330 seen here in its original dark blue-grey colour with white lightning flash and titles added. The photograph shows XM330 visiting Cranfield on 9 March 1973. (Photo: Dick Winfield)

(Bottom:) The same Wessex HAS.1, XM330, photographed four years later repainted in the 'raspberry ripple' scheme, while displayed at Blackbushe on 30 July 1977. (Photo: Stephen Wolf)

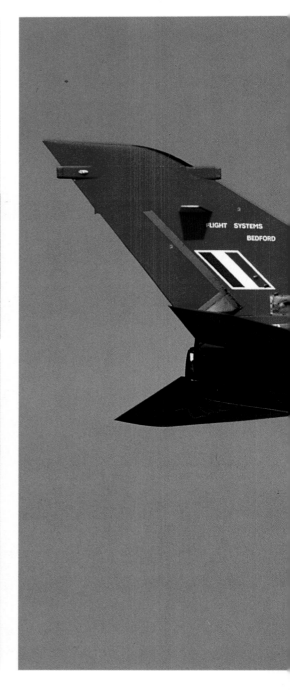

(Below:) The sole Tornado to be painted in 'raspberry ripple' is GR.IT, ZA326, which currently operates with the Flight Systems Division at RAE Bedford. It had its rear end damaged in a production line fire at Warton and was deferred from entering squadron service. After a rebuild, it entered service with the RAE in 1983. Among other trials, it has been used for laser terrain following trials. The photograph shows ZA326 during its first public appearance, landing at Fairford on 21 July 1989 for the International Air Tattoo. (Photo: Adrian Balch)

(Below:) Vickers V.837 Viscount, XT575 was built at Weybridge and first flew as OE-LAG, being delivered to Austrian Airlines on 29 February 1960 named 'Franz Schubert'. In August 1964 it was sold to the Ministry of Technology and delivered to RRE Pershore on 31 October 1964 as XT575. Fitted with a large radome under the forward fuselage, XT575 was rolled out at Pershore with blue cheatline and matt red rear fuselage and fin. XT575 moved to Bedford in April 1977, when Pershore closed and was repainted in the 'raspberry ripple' colour scheme by 1983. Used for radar trials by the Radar Signals Research Squadron of RAE, it was finally withdrawn from use in 1990 and, at the time of writing, was in open store at Bedford. The photograph shows XT575 in the static park at Fairford on 12 July 1985, during the International Air Tattoo. (Photo: Adrian Balch)

(Right:) The last airworthy Vickers Varsity was WL679, seen here over RAE Farnborough, which made its final flight on 2 August 1991. It was delivered to RAE Farnborough's Radio Flight in January 1954, being transferred to RRE Pershore in August 1968, then returned to RAE at Farnborough, when Pershore closed in April 1977. Until March 1985 WL679 wore an aluminium finish with white roof, separated by a broad medium blue cheatline. After this date, it adopted the familiar 'raspberry ripple' scheme shown here. In 1992, it was transferred to the Cosford Aerospace Museum. (Photo: RAE)

De Havilland Sea Vixen D.3, XS577, is one of a pair of drones currently operated by RAE Llanbedr. It was planned to convert several Sea Vixens to drone configuration, to replace Llanbedr's Meteors, but due to budget restrictions only four were converted for target-tug and drone work by Flight Refuelling Ltd at Tarrant Rushton. Only two went into service, being XP924 and XS577. Although the Sea Vixen D.3s were basically painted red and yellow each had slightly different variations on the theme. The photograph shows XS577 at Bournemouth-Hurn on 20 July 1980. (Photo: Stephen Wolf)

Vickers VC-10, XX914, began life as an order for Ghana Airways as 9G-ABQ, but was never delivered. It went to British United Airways on 1 July 1965 as G-ATDJ and was subsequently merged into the British Caledonian Airways fleet in September 1971, being named 'Loch Fyne'. It was sold to the Ministry of Technology in March 1973, for use by RAE Bedford as a testbed and flying laboratory, becoming XX914. It was withdrawn from use in July 1983 and broken up at Bedford, the fuselage going to the Air Movements School at Brize Norton as 8777M. Throughout its RAE service XX914 wore the smart red and yellow trim seen here. (Photo: RAE Bedford)

(Right:) One of the four Sikorsky-built SH-3D Sea Kings delivered prior to licence production was XV371, which currently serves with DRA Farnborough in the 'raspberry ripple' scheme. It is seen here in its original dark blue scheme with strip dayglo trim in July 1976. (Photo: RAE)

(Below:) Westland Sea King Mk.4X, ZB507, currently serves with the DRA at Farnborough and is seen here on standby fire duties during the Farnborough Air Show in September 1990. (Photo: Adrian Balch)

(Left:) H.S. Andover C.1 (mod), XS646, currently serves with the RAE at Farnborough, using a multi-lens infra-red camera nose with Vinten camera pod under the nose, replacing Varsity WL679, which has been retired. It appears that one 'pig' has replaced another! These photographs were taken at Boscombe Down during Air Tournament '92. (Photos: Adrian Balch)

(Right top:) Folland Gnat T.1, XP505, served with the RAE at Bedford on gust and turbulence research using the nose and wingtip probes. It was delivered to Bedford in May 1969 and was sold to the Science Museum on 29 April 1983. It was installed in the museum at South Kensington, London, in November 1984, but was moved to the museum's outstation at Wroughton, Wiltshire, in late 1992. It is seen here at Abingdon on 18 September 1982, with RAE BAC One-Eleven, XX105, behind. (Photo: John Hughes)

(Right bottom:) Westland Wessex, XL728, was a hybrid Mk.1 upgraded to Mk.5 standard with the latter's exhaust outlet. It was the second pre-production Wessex and served all its life with RAE Farnborough. It is seen in the smart white grey and blue RAE scheme at Farnborough on 10 September 1972. Towards the end of its life, it was repainted in the 'raspberry ripple' scheme, being retired in 1985 to the Pendine Ranges, where it was destroyed. (Photo: Stephen Wolf)

(Below:) XW241 was the first Puma to wear British military markings, being an Aerospatiale-built machine sent to Westlands for trials in 1970. It was later passed on to the RAE at Bedford, where it gained an instrumentation nose probe and was subsequently given the 'raspberry ripple' treatment. It served at Farnborough and Bedford until 9 August 1991 when it was in the South of France engaged in trials, during which it caught fire and crashed, killing all on board. (Photo: RAE Bedford)

(Opposite:) Westland Puma HC.1, ZA941, has been in service with RAE Farnborough's Experimental Flying Squadron since the autumn of 1981 and is the last British military Puma to be produced. (Photo: Westland)

(Left:) Meteor NF.14, WS838, banks away from the camera-ship over RAE Bedford in 1971, revealing its underwing serials and grey port and centreline fuel tanks.

(Below:) After service with the RAF, Gloster Meteor NF.14, WS838, was transferred to the Ministry of Supply on 1 November 1961 and started eleven years of test work. This was undertaken with the All Weather Wing, followed by the Royal Radar Establishment at Pershore, then with A&AEE at Boscombe Down and finally with the RAE at Bedford. It was retired in late 1971 and earmarked for the RAF Museum, total flying time having amounted to 1,900 hours. It was delivered to the Colerne Museum in February 1972, then was roaded to Shawbury on Colerne's closure on 11 September 1975 and was on display at Cosford in time for the Aerospace Museum's first open day of the 1976 season, in April. It was later transferred to the Midland Air Museum at Coventry, where it can be seen today. This superb top view shows the markings to advantage and was taken in 1971 just before retirement from RAE Bedford. (Photos: RAE)

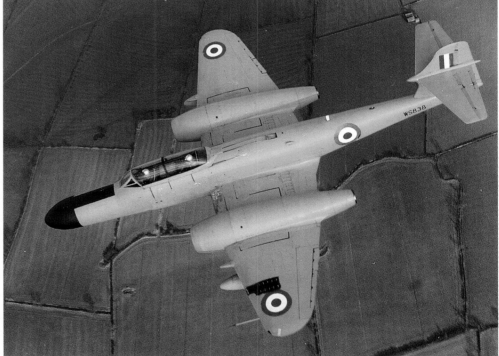

(Right:) A good top-side view of Canberra T.4, WJ992, from RAE Bedford on 16 November 1977. This Canberra served with RRE Pershore from January 1957 until moving to Bedford in April 1977. It last flew on 1 April 1993.

(Below:) WT327 is a B(I)8 fitted with a B.2 nose and was transferred from RAF charge on 9 December 1955 to Ferranti for radar trials. It then went to RRE Pershore in a silver and dayglo scheme and was transferred to RAE Bedford in 1977, adopting the 'raspberry ripple' scheme seen here and was still flying in these colours in 1991. This photograph was taken near Bedford on 25 March 1988. (Photos: RAE Bedford)

(Below:) RAE Farnborough's Comet 4, XV814, showing its newly painted 'raspberry ripple' scheme in March 1977. This was the penultimate airworthy Comet in the world, being retired from service in January 1993 and used for spares at Boscombe Down to keep XS235 flying.
(Photo: RAE)

(Right:) This unique formation took place in April 1972 over the Bedfordshire countryside to mark the retirement of the one and only Comet 3B from active flying. The British airline industry owes much to two of these three aircraft for the immense amount of radio and blind landing development work that has taken place in them. Leading the formation is the oldest of the three aircraft, XN453. Built as G-AMXD, c/n 06026, this aircraft was the fourth Comet 2 for BOAC

and appeared in 1954, the year that all the Comets were grounded. It was re-engined and was re-designated Comet 2E. After route-proving trials by BOAC, it was taken over by RAE Farnborough and reworked as a radio workshop. Since 1959, it has flown the world on the development of long-range radio-navigation aids until being withdrawn from use in February 1973, when it was scrapped at Farnborough. In the Number 2 position is XP915, possibly the most important Comet of all. It started life as G-ANLO, c/n 06100, the one and only Comet 3. The success of the subsequent Comet Mk.4 was due to all the development and route-proving trials by the Comet 3. This aircraft was re-engineered with the Comet 4B wing for the projected BEA version and was used for all this model's development flying. On 21 June 1961 G-ANLO became XP915 and was transferred to

RAE Bedford for the Blind Landing Experimental Unit. It was withdrawn from use in March 1972 and was used for ground tests into braking systems. On 22 August 1973 it was transferred to Woodford by road for use as a Nimrod test rig. Nearest aircraft in the photograph is XV814, which had a more pedestrian beginning than the other two, being delivered to BOAC on the last day of 1958 as G-APDF, c/n 6407, the sixth production Comet 4. It served with BOAC until 1967, when it was bought by the Ministry for research flying. Intended to carry on and extend the work done by XN453 over the years, it was probably the most modified of all the Comets. The large pannier under the nose provided an equipment bay for the work to be carried out and to offset this extra keel area forward, the aircraft was flown to Woodford where it was fitted with a Nimrod fin.

(Right:) XP831 was the first prototype Hawker P.1127, and was the first aircraft from which the Harrier family stemmed. Following development work with Bristol Siddeley and Hawkers, it went to the Aerodynamics Flight at RAE Bedford in 1965 and remained there until being withdrawn from use in 1972. It was transferred by road to the RAF Museum at Hendon on 13 November 1972, where it was on display for twenty years until going on loan to the Science Museum at South Kensington in 1992. (Photo: RAE Bedford)

(Below:) BAC One-Eleven 479FU, ZE433, seen at RAE Bedford on 2 May 1984, still wearing the colours of Air Pacific of Fiji, to whom it was previously registered DQ-FBQ.

(Bottom:) The same aircraft pictured on 2 December 1987 in service with RAE Bedford, now fitted with a Sea Harrier FRS.2 nose for Blue Vixen radar trials. (Photos: RAE Bedford)

METEOROLOGICAL RESEARCH FLIGHT AT RAE FARNBOROUGH

(Below:) WE173 was the last Canberra operated by the Meteorological Research Flight at Farnborough. Built as a PR.3, WE173 was given a long instrumental nose probe for gust and turbulence research. Initially flying in an overall silver finish, by 1972 it was painted white and light grey with red trim. The nose probe was painted in red and white hoops. When the Met. Research Flight's Hercules W.2 entered service in 1973, WE173 was soon made redundant, being withdrawn from use on 31 March 1981. It went to the fire dump at Coltishall on 4 March 1982 and was still there in 1991. The photograph shows Canberra PR.3, WE173, visiting Lyneham on 20 September 1972 during one of its weather research flights. (Photo: Adrian Balch)

The history of the Meteorological Research Flight can be traced back some forty-five years to the establishment of a research programme with aircraft of the High Altitude Flight based at Boscombe Down. The meteorological reconnaissance missions that were being flown during the war did not have the benefit of our present understanding of the physical properties of the atmosphere. Accurate weather forecasting was vital to the success of all large scale military operations and the Meteorological Research Committee was formed in November 1941 to consider means of improving existing meteorological techniques. They recognized the value of

carrying instrumentation to high altitudes and urgently requested that aircraft be allocated specially for meteorological research. All the necessary arrangements had been made by August 1942 and a meteorologist was assigned to Boscombe Down to take control of a programme of research flying by aircraft of the High Altitude Flight. A Boston and two Spitfires initially equipped the Flight, but they were soon joined by a Mosquito, Hudson and B-17 as the research progressed.

The Flight's task was to conduct atmospheric research and to refine and improve the techniques and instrumentation in use at that time; weather forecasting was not

part of the job. Early trials involved developing instruments to accurately measure the temperature and humidity of air from high speed aircraft. The success of the Flight, even under wartime conditions, was such that it was given a more permanent home and a name that confirmed its status as a self-contained scientific research unit. It became known as the Meteorological Research Flight (MRF) in August 1946 and moved from Boscombe Down to its permanent base at RAE Farnborough, now DRA.

Following its move to Farnborough, the MRF was equipped with two Mosquito PR.34s and two Halifax Mk.6s. These aircraft retained their operational camouflage

colours and no special colour scheme was thought to have been carried.

Strictly speaking, the Meteorological Research Flight is a lodger unit at Farnborough, with no direct ties of 'ownership' between the RAE and the MRF. The MRF is actually a unit of the Meteorological Office and forms part of the Directorate of Research; it reports directly to the Deputy Director of Physical Research at nearby Bracknell and the twenty-five or so civilian staff are employed by the Meteorological Office. The Royal Air Force supplies the aircraft and the skilled aircrew necessary for this kind of operation. The aircraft used in the last twenty years are as follows:

HANDLEY PAGE HASTINGS C.1A, TG618

The exact delivery date is unknown, but by 1963 the MRF was operating Hastings C.1A, TG618, fitted with an instrumentation pod under its nose. Apart from the standard transport scheme of silver and white, the tailplanes, propeller spinners and most of the fin were painted dayglo orange. Meteorological Research Flight titles appeared on the cabin roof in black letters. The Hastings remained in service until the late 1960s and was scrapped at Farnborough in July/August 1969.

VICKERS VARSITY T.1, WJ906.

After service with No.3 Air Navigation School, Varsity T.1, WJ906, joined the Hastings with the MRF during the early 1960s. Initially the nose, rear fuselage and fin were painted dayglo orange, while the rest of the airframe was silver with a white cabin roof divided by a Transport Command-style dark blue cheatline. However, by 1969, the fin and rear fuselage above the cheatline had been repainted white. WJ906 served the MRF until it was officially struck off charge on 4 May 1970 and sent to the Manston Fire School.

VICKERS VARSITY T.1, WF425.

When WJ906 was retired, the MRF was immediately allocated a replacement Varsity in the form of WF425. This machine had previously served with 2 ANS, 1 ANS and the Central Flying School, before joining the MRF on 24 March 1970. WF425 had an interchangeable nose cone with small air sampling probes inserted into it. The aircraft was painted light grey and white with dayglo red ranels on the nose, rear fuselage and fin. It served with the Flight until withdrawn from use in 1974, when it was replaced by the current Hercules W.2. WF425 was acquired by the Imperial War Museum and flown to Duxford for static display, where it resides today.

ENGLISH ELECTRIC CANBERRA PR-3, WE173.

Canberra PR-3, WE173, was delivered to the MRF in 1965 in an overall-silver finish. It was fitted with a 15ft nose-probe to

ensure that several sensitive instruments contained therein were kept well clear of the airflow disturbances created by the aircraft itself. The Canberra was primarily used for work in the stratosphere (above about 35,000ft) and retained its silver finish until 1972, when it was repainted in a smart colour scheme of light grey and white, with a red cheatline and red/white nose-probe. In this form, WE173 continued with the MRF for another ten years, including a 2½-month detachment to Colorado early in 1973, to study mountain-induced airflow. The aircraft also spent some time at Dakar, Senegal, in November 1975 to enable radiometer experiments to be made in tropical regions. WE173 was withdrawn from use during 1982 and ended its days with RAF Coltishall's Fire Section.

LOCKHEED HERCULES W.2, XV208.

The C-130K Hercules aircraft, currently used by the MRF, has been re-designated from the original C.Mk.1 to the more appropriate W.Mk.2. The aircraft joined the RAF on 22 September 1967 and was delivered to No.48 Squadron, Far East Air Force, at Changi, Singapore for the first part of its life. It was decided to replace the MRF's Hastings and Varsity aircraft with a single, more modern mount. The Hercules was selected as being the most practical type for the tasks involved.

After extensive modification by Marshalls of Cambridge, XV208 was finally delivered to the MRF on 3 January 1974. The most obvious modifications are the 22ft nose-probe, the re-positioned radome and the extra pair of fuel tanks outboard of the engines, which are the same as those fitted to C-130A models. The paint scheme is fairly simple, with the main bulk of the fuselage, wings and tailplanes being light grey. The fuselage top and fin are white, with a thin medium-blue cheatline running down the fuselage. Like the Canberra, the Hercules has its nose probe striped red and white.

As the MRF is only a 'lodger' unit at Farnborough, the Hercules is not expected to adopt the MoD(PE) 'raspberry ripple' colour scheme and should continue in the same scheme for the rest of its life.

THE MOVE TO BOSCOMBE DOWN

As this is written, the airfields at Bedford and Farnborough are expected to close, with all aircraft fleets transferring to Boscombe Down. This is due to drastic reductions in military research and development programmes, which will mean that all research and development flying activity will be concentrated at A&AEE Boscombe Down. This announcement was made by Parliamentary Under Secretary of State for Defence Kenneth Carlisle on 9 May 1991. The two establishments are now under the Defence Research Agency, which currently has its headquarters at Farnborough.

The new location for the MRF has yet to be decided.

The Meteorological Research Flight operated Vickers Varsity T.1, WF425, from 24 March 1970 until it was sold to Duxford for preservation on 20 May 1975. Flying from Farnborough, it was painted white and light grey with red dayglo strips. The nose cone could be detached and replaced by one with air sampling pipes. WF425 is seen here visiting Lyneham on 4 June 1974. (Photo: Adrian Balch)